TRAINING GAMES

STEVE SUGAR
JENNIFER WHITCOMB

PRESS

Simple and Effective Techniques
To Engage and Motivate Learners

ASTD Press is an internationally renowned source of insightful and practical information on workplace learning and performance topics, including training basics, evaluation and return-on-investment (ROI), instructional systems development (ISD), e-learning, leadership, and career development.

Ordering information: Books published by ASTD Press can be purchased by visiting our Website at store.astd.org or by calling 800.628.2783 or 703.683.8100.

Library of Congress Control Number: 2006923213

ISBN-10: 1-56286-451-3
ISBN-13: 978-1-56286-451-4

Acquisitions and Development Editor: Mark Morrow
Copyeditor: Christine Cotting
Interior Design and Production: Kathleen Schaner
Cover Design: Ana Ilieva
Cover Illustration: Kazu Nitta

Contents

Preface

♦

I stand here singing my song. You leave here singing it . . . I hope.
—Anonymous

♦

As trainers, our goal is to make the training event memorable, whether the topic is assigned to us or is one we've chosen. As we assemble our lesson plan, we must design not only the "what" (or content), but also the "how" (the delivery mechanisms) so that the learner interacts with key concepts at the prescribed level, ranging from basic understanding to real-life work applications.

In writing this book, our premise is simple—we recommend that you include training games in your existing tool kit of exercises, techniques, stories, and training aids. Think about it . . .

♦ Games are familiar. We've played them since childhood. We're comfortable in assuming player roles and following the rules of familiar games, such as bingo, as we seek out the topic information needed to complete the game requirements.

♦ Games are energizers. They celebrate the topic in a smiling, nonthreatening learning zone. Games invite players to enter into friendly competition where both successes and mistakes are shared learning moments.

♦ Games are interactive. Today's learner needs to try things on his or her own, and games bring the learner into direct contact with the topic in such a way that he or she receives immediate feedback on quality of input in a play-and-learn experience.

Here's a case in point: Sister Cecelia, the hospital's director of training, was concerned with the orientation training. For one thing, the training session was a series of dull personnel lectures to new hires, who listened politely but never asked questions. More troubling, however, was the continuous stream of new hires returning to the human resource office with questions about the same information presented during the orientation. This not only created additional work for the personnel staff, but also took new hires away from their assignments.

Sr. Cecelia decided to introduce an information search game called "Orientation Bingo." New employees entering the training room each received a packet of information, a pencil, and a bingo game sheet containing clue words in each of the 25 squares. When Sr. Cecelia opened the program, she explained that the bingo sheets held clues concerning key information that would be covered during the orientation sessions. She invited the participants to write the number of the presentation in the appropriate square and then mark an "X" through the completed square. She explained that the first three participants who completely filled in their bingo game sheets would win their choice of a hospital coffee mug or baseball cap. Here's the game sheet Sr. Cecelia designed for use in the new hires' orientation:

Orientation Bingo Game Sheet

Wound Care	Fit Testing	Visiting Hours	Outpatient	Housekeeping
Diabetes Management	Burn Center	Code Protocol	Lab Clothes	Incident Report
Emergency Services	Resus	Personal Leave	Dietary	Customer Service
Infection Control	Education	Radiology	Utilization Review	Shift Hours
EKG	Cafeteria Hours	Stat	Badges	Admitting

Well, let us assure you—that hospital's orientation training has never been the same! Now new employees look forward to each presentation and, bingo sheets in hand, they ask questions, seek out information and, once in a while, even shout "Bingo!" Everyone seems to be happy with the new training, especially the human resource staff whose after-training duties have returned to normal.

Introducing the Orientation Bingo game was successful at several levels:

◆ *For the participants:* The new hires immediately took to the game. The format was familiar, and making a connection between a clue and a presentation was more fun than task. Participants were energized and smiling, eagerly awaiting the next clue to complete their quest. But, most important, they interacted with the material—often asking questions to ensure they made the correct clue associations.

◆ *For human resource personnel:* Besides enjoying the lessened workload that usually followed the orientation training, the HR speakers took on a renewed interest in the quality of their presentations. Although several speakers attributed this renewed interest as a natural reaction to anticipated audience questions, it was easy to detect a greater anticipation of the actual orientation event—as if the speakers shared the increased energy and excitement of the event.

◆ *For the hospital:* Many departments reported higher productivity among new employees, noting that they seemed less distracted and more comfortable in their new work environment.

This was a positive game experience for all concerned. But it didn't "just happen"—it took thoughtful planning and timely preparation to create the event. To make this event happen, Sr. Cecelia executed these action steps:

◆ *Prior to the event,*
 — She selected a well-known, easily played game format (bingo).
 — She collected key information from each presentation.
 — She assigned each presentation a number (using the three-digit telephone extension of the presenter).
 — She created the bingo game sheets, placing clue words and phrases in each square.
 — She printed the bingo game sheets.
 — She gathered the prizes.
◆ *On the day of the event,*
 — She introduced the game, creating a game-friendly environment.
 — She administered the game, verifying the winning game sheets and awarding prizes.

It is just this kind of experience that we want to help you have at each of your training sessions. First we're going to encourage you to take a leap of faith and try a game—and then we're going to give you the preparatory help you need to "make it happen" just like Sr. Cecelia.

The Book at a Glance

The goal of this book is not only to inspire you to use a training game, but to give you the information and the techniques to create your own positive game experience.

Use the first seven chapters of this book as an overview of the introduction, selection, preparation, play, and debriefing of training games. Then preview the Game Use Matrix in chapter 8 to help you select one of the games in that chapter that suits your particular topic and audience.

Use chapters 1, 4, and 6 to consider the basics of classroom games, the four game formats, the role of the game facilitator, and how David Kolb's Experiential Learning Cycle affects your training.

Chapters 2 and 3 address game development. Use them to consider the issues involved in first selecting and then developing and preparing your game for play.

Making a game selection is covered in chapters 2, 4, and 8. Use them to examine the options available in selecting your game—including an overview of the four game formats. Then select one of the 11 classroom games presented in detail there.

Study chapters 3 and 5 to learn about game setup. Use them as a working guide to developing and preparing your game materials, making necessary pre-game preparations, and then playing your game.

Chapters 6 and 7 cover the roles and responsibilities of the facilitator and the techniques for debriefing the game. Use them to put yourself into the facilitator role and to create a meaningful debriefing that reveals and reinforces lessons learned in play.

Use chapter 8 as a source for field-tested, easy-to-adapt classroom games. First look at the Game Use Matrix to see which game(s) will fit your training objectives. Then use the detailed instructions for the game(s) you select.

The CD-ROM that accompanies this book has electronic copies of the game sheets and player instructions. Use these to print copies for use in your training sessions.

So, we welcome you to *Training Games* and hope you find the book your ever-ready reference and resource.

Let the games begin!

Steve Sugar
Jennifer Whitcomb
June 2006

Acknowledgments

Thanks to ASTD's acquisitions editor Mark Morrow, designer Kathleen Schaner, and proofreader Kris Paternaude, all of whom made this project happen—and special thanks to our editor, Christine Cotting, whose guidance and gentle humor turned a manuscript into a book.

This is for the trainers who create magic moments every day in organization classrooms all over the world.

Introduction to Training Games

Teach me half the gladness that thy brain must know...
—Percy B. Shelley, "To a Skylark"

For a moment, imagine all your learners keenly focused on your topic question as they lean forward to hear the correct answer and then react accordingly—with celebrations if their responses are correct, or with stoic acknowledgment of incorrect responses. Then imagine a series of such golden "learning moments," woven into a tapestry that reflects the key points of your training plan. *This* is what a training game can bring to your training arena.

Training games, learning games, classroom games, performance games—whatever you call them—are a delightful way to bring key topic areas to your learner. The payoff is two "ways to learn." First, the game brings energy and involvement to even the driest of topics; and second, participants display real-time game-play behavior that translates into meaningful post-game debriefing dialogue.

This book is designed to help you succeed in using games in your classroom—it's your guide to training games, beginning with a discussion of the techniques and processes required to develop, administer, and process your training game experience. We also offer a "starter set" of 11 training games. Each of these game designs has been played successfully with the most demanding and critical audience we know—today's learner. From these field tests we have compiled trainer and player instructions and notes to help you set up, play, and debrief each game.

The 11 games, which should cover your every gaming need, include

* an icebreaker favorite (Signature Hunt)
* an energizing information search (Review Bingo)
* a topic review quiz (Quiz Challenge)
* a familiar format adapted for topic review (Tic-Tac-Topic)
* a test-and-target-toss topic review (Toss Up)
* a playful sorting contest (Card Sort)
* two team creativity activities (Bingo Hunt and Match Point)
* a team-learning review (Get-Set)
* a team problem-solving/risk-taking floor game (Sand Trap)
* a fast-moving team board game (Board Bingo).

Ten Reasons Why Games Are "HOT" (High-Outcome Techniques)

Successful training games are easy to describe—they're simple in design and simply fun to play. A successful game can energize almost any content and produce powerful new understanding for your trainees. Games promote learning—more than just introducing a playful environment or creating a challenge between the topic and the participant, they create opportunities for the learner to "interact" with the game so as to demonstrate her or his understanding of the topic, through such means as information recall and experiential application.

Reason #1: Games Are Fun With a Purpose

A game creates a cognitive interaction between the learner and the topic in a buoyant environment. Games celebrate your topic and reward individual and group achievement. With a focus on learning, they bring fun and energy into the room, and put the joy of discovery back into the learning process.

Reason #2: Games Give Learners Valuable Feedback

Learners need and want feedback on their performance. Games give them immediate feedback on the quality of their actions—both their successes and their errors. With the appropriate corrective feedback, this can be an invaluable learning opportunity.

Reason #3: Games Give Trainers Feedback

By observing learners playing a real-time game and demonstrating their knowledge of and ability in a topic, the trainer can discover how to adjust the subsequent training accordingly—the level of lecture, the nature of assigned readings or outside work, and the kinds of intervention that will be needed.

Reason #4: Games Are Experiential

Today's learner needs to do and to try things on his or her own. Games create an environment that transforms the passive student into an active part of the learning process. Here the learner can connect his or her own dots and experience his or her own ideas. Games also remind both player and trainer that energy in the classroom is a good thing.

Reason #5: Games Motivate Learners

A game engages the learner and then motivates him or her to examine the topic. This drives your learners to demonstrate their understanding of the topic in a friendly contest where successes are memorable moments of shared triumph and celebration and where mistakes mean only that the learner is stretching his or her own limits. And trainers can use the time following game play to build a bridge between the topic and the learner. Because games are played and experienced in real time, observed behavior and participant feelings can be revisited and reviewed for continuing insights.

Reason #6: Games Improve Team Work

When a game or activity involves team play, then it becomes a real-time event that brings players into focused groups, demonstrates the rules and roles of working together as a team, and underscores the value of collaboration. Games give your learners a chance to get to know their peers as they share the same real-time experiences, and this promotes strong networking and bonding inside the training room and back in the workplace.

Reason #7: Games Lower the Threat Level in the Learning Environment

Games provide a practice field where players learn that making mistakes is just part of the game, and where they find they learn as much from errors as from successes. Game play reminds us that everything in life—both at work and at home—involves trial and error, and moving on.

Reason #8: Games Reveal Real-World Relevance

A game enables you to present real-world information in the form of questions, scenarios, and role plays. It helps you connect your topic to the work world in which your players operate every day. Players learn not only the "what" but also the "why" of the topic from a practical perspective. They also observe their own real-time behaviors and those of others during game play. Post-game debriefings give insights into those behaviors in thoughtful examples observed during game play.

Reason #9: Games Accelerate Learning

With a game you can compress your topic and demonstrated learning into shorter periods of time, thereby accelerating the speed of learning. The visual presentation, verbal interactions, and physical action of game play appeal to all of the participants' learning styles (visual, auditory, and kinesthetic). And by involving both the rational and experiential areas of the brain, game play helps players remember what they have learned.

Reason #10: Games Give You Choices for Your Classroom

Games let you add variety and flexibility to your instructional menu by varying

- the level of learner involvement
- the level of skill and knowledge required
- the level of play to suit an audience of any size
- the type and level of activity
- the level of classroom control
- the perspective—that is, you may introduce a topic, review a topic, or both
- the mix of theoretical and practical information.

Case in Point

Using Tic-Tac-Topic as a Pretest

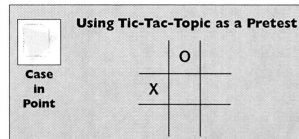

Trainer's Purpose: To gain an early baseline reading on how much the participants know and understand about the topic

Step 1: Divide the whole class into two teams—"X" and "O."

Step 2: Draw the familiar tic-tac-toe grid on a flipchart or overhead transparency.

Step 3: At random, ask one player from the "X" team to select a space on the grid.

Step 4: Present your first topic question.

— If the randomly selected player's response is correct, mark an "X" on the selected space.
— If the response is incorrect, leave the space open.

Step 5: Select a player from the "O" side and repeat Step 4.

Step 6: Repeat the random selection and question-and-answer process until one team has its mark in three spaces in a row.

After a few rounds of game play, you have a pretty clear idea of how much your learners know about the topic under consideration, and you've started them thinking about the topic.

For more information on preparing, playing, and debriefing this game, see Tic-Tac-Topic in chapter 8.

Fear of Failure

You may fear that a training game will fail in its promise to create a motivated and better-informed learner. If the three key words in real estate are "location, location, location," then the three-word mantra for using a training game in your lesson is "preparation, preparation, preparation." Here's an action plan to minimize most of your first-game risks, and a discussion of additional activities you'll need to make time for as you prepare for a game.

Action Plan for Avoiding Failure

Review your lesson plan and note where a game will fit well with the topic.

* Develop a short list of expectations. For example, the game should
  — review major learning points
  — demonstrate each learner's level of topic understanding
  — establish a baseline reading on how much the learners comprehend about your topic, as demonstrated in the quality of their responses during game play.
* Select a game format that you feel matches your topic and your audience. (How to make this selection will be covered in greater detail in chapter 2.)
* Develop a list of questions that cover your learning points; depending on the game format, the question set can range from 10 to 30 questions.
* Become familiar with the selected game by
  — reviewing the game's rules of play
  — inserting your questions into the format and, if possible, playing a sample round in solitaire fashion
  — if possible, conducting a pilot session with colleagues.
* Review your training plan to ensure that you have created a flow into your game, and then a flow back to your training plan.
* Create a *Before-During-After* timeline for your game.
  — *Before* (25 percent of the time allotted to the game in your lesson plan): Create a climate for the game experience, introduce the game, form teams, and distribute materials.
  — *During* (50 percent of the time allotted): Conduct the game, including clarifying the rules, the questions, and time expectations as needed.
  — *After* (25 percent of the time): Discuss the game in terms of what happened, what real-time behaviors contributed to the success or failure of game play, and what learning experiences (information and behaviors) relate to the topic and the workplace.

Additional Preparatory Steps

Introducing any new training experience—be it survey instruments, activities, even PowerPoint presentations—requires additional time. For a game, these extra activities are needed:

- *Preparation:* Inserting the game into your training plan; preparing question sets; (optionally) creating presentation materials in PowerPoint, on overhead transparencies, or on flipchart pages
- *Game Materials:* Preparing game sheets or boards, question cards, and handouts; locating accessories and props
- *Logistics:* Securing classroom audio-visual equipment; arranging tables and chairs
- *Delivery Preparation:* Familiarizing yourself with the rules and your role as game administrator; preparing key points to cover when introducing and debriefing game play.

These preparations may seem overwhelming, but they are not too different from the preparing you'd have to do for any new training intervention. Most games require from two to seven minutes of preparation for each minute of classroom play—for example, a 20-minute game will require from 40 to 140 minutes to prepare. But, once you have successfully introduced the game the first time, you'll need about 20 percent less preparation for subsequent uses. When you've done the original preparation, you have a well-planned learning experience that anchors your module and enables you to build additional application of major learning concepts into the training design.

The Basics: What Is a Training Game?

A training or learning game is any game from which participants can learn something of value. It's a rule-governed activity that requires player input. For example, our rule for Tic-Tac-Topic is that a player has to answer a question correctly before he or she can claim a space for the team—therefore, the player has to earn the space with his or her input. Instructional games usually, but not always, include some form of competition.

Five Elements of a Training Game

We turned the traditional tic-tac-toe format into an instructional game by adding the element of topic information. That's one of the game elements we'll talk about here. And there are four other elements you can add to a quiz to produce a training game. Let's look at Quiz Challenge, a quiz made into a game, as we discuss each of the five elements of a training game: contest, interaction, structure, outcome, and topic information.

Element 1: Contest

A *contest* is a competition against other players (opponents) or against a standard (for example, time, or the quantity or quality of responses). Perhaps the contest or challenge is the most crucial part of a game because it's the hook that encourages the learner to become a player.

Quiz Challenge

Make a game out of an ordinary quiz by challenging the players to estimate their correct responses *before* they take the quiz. Asking "How many content questions will you correctly answer in this seven-question quiz?" gets your learner interested in both the question and the quality of his or her answers in the quest to match his or her pre-quiz estimate.

Element 2: Interaction

Interaction in gaming is the ongoing dynamics of play among the participants (and sometimes between the facilitator and each participant). It also refers to the way in which players react to and behave with the game rules, and what they do with the topic information they're meant to learn.

Quiz Challenge

The "challenge," given prior to an ordinary quiz, creates an immediate interaction between the players and the topic, between players on two-person teams, and between players/teams and the rules of the game as learners try to match their pre-quiz estimates.

Element 3: Structure

The format that states the "how" of the game—the rules and roles of play—is the *structure*. It tells the players what they can do, what they can't do, who is winning and losing (when relevant), and when the game is over.

Quiz Challenge

Players are instructed first to estimate how many correct responses they will make to seven questions, and then to complete the task of responding to seven questions within the specified time (10 minutes).

Element 4: Outcome

The *outcome* of play varies in detail from game to game, but generally involves winning by accomplishing some goal or task (building a model or completing a crossword puzzle) or by matching or beating a standard (such as time, or quantity or quality of responses).

> **Quiz Challenge**
>
> At the end of the question review, players tally their correct responses. The team that matches or beats members' original estimate is declared the winner. (If Team A estimated six correct responses and then answered seven questions correctly, then Team A is the winner or one of the winning teams.)

Element 5: Topic Information

The *topic information* to be applied or demonstrated during game play is the learning element of a game.

> **Quiz Challenge**
>
> During Quiz Challenge, each player's interest is driven by his or her need to know (a) if his or her response was correct or incorrect, and (b) why. Although a player's initial focus may be on scoring, his or her interest in the topic increases with the presentation of each question, and this creates "teachable moments" in which players are more receptive to both the correct response and the rationale behind the selection.

A Game Is More Than a Learning Activity

A "learning activity" is a dynamic classroom exercise that promotes learning by doing—observable physical behavior. All games are activities, but not all activities are games. The differences are in the structure, outcome, and scoring. Although an activity has interaction (between or among players), and outcome (task-specific results), it's not structured (measured and scored) like a game. Furthermore, a game usually is driven by designed-in competition that typically is not found in an activity.

Our Quiz Challenge game differs from an ordinary question-and-answer session because it creates a competitive "challenge" between players and their own personal estimates and among the different playing groups (teams).

Activities are dynamic and/or kinesthetic alternatives to lecture and they include

- icebreakers
- panels or debates
- guided notetaking/journaling
- role plays
- team teaching
- in-baskets
- fishbowl
- brainstorming
- simulations

- closers
- video, DVD, and audio clips
- interviews
- coaching
- skits and scriptwriting
- round-robin discussions
- art or graphic projects
- consensus decision making
- case studies
- instructional puzzles.

Games Differ From Simulations

A simulation is a practice field for a simplified real-world situation where participants experience conditions that correspond to real life, make decisions, and get feedback about the consequences of their decisions. A "simple" simulation is the familiar "In-Basket" exercise, an activity requiring participants to sort and prioritize a stack of managerial paperwork. Each participant's results are then reviewed in terms of how well the papers were prioritized and/or processed.

There are also "complicated" simulations that carefully correspond to fully developed systems or subsystems of a real-world model, process, or equipment, such as airline pilot simulators. Here the participant "enters" the real-life situation and is evaluated on the quality and timing of his or her responses.

Simulations have definite structure (rules and norms) and required engagement between participant and task, and they focus on specific outcomes (successful completion of task). But simulations lack the "playfulness" of a game, are often very complex, and are measured on degrees of success and failure rather than scores or "win-lose."

Case in Point

Simulation Example: Cocktail Conversations

Lu Key Products had a reputation for conducting a grueling international training program. First the candidates had to pass a rigorous battery of assessments and knowledge tests, and then participate in a series of individual and group interviews. The last hurdle required the candidates to attend a "cocktail party" for their buyers and suppliers from the Frankfort region. Here the candidates not only had to deal with conversing in a mix of English and German, but also were subjected to conversations regarding cultural awareness, local history, and current politics.

It was no secret that those candidates who were the most comfortable and tactful during these cocktail conversations were the first ones selected for the next available overseas assignments.

Simulations include

* real-world applications exercise
* business models
* airplane, ship, and other transportation simulators
* in-basket exercises
* role plays
* case studies involving direct participation.

Decision Steps for Selecting a Game

Where do you begin to choose the right game for your training session? Let's take a look at five steps that will guide you in your game selection.

Step 1: Identify Your Training Session's Ultimate Objective

The decision of "to game or not to game" begins with the end product in mind. Specifically, what skills, knowledge, and/or attitudes do you want your learners to take home from the presentation? The outcome can be specific (for example, explain how to give feedback to direct reports, or list potential safety hazards), or the outcome can be global (perhaps, create interest in a training event such as hospital orientation). Think about the final or overall objective for the training and how the game will help participants meet the overall objective. Within the parameters of your training module, how does the game help meet the module or unit objectives?

Sometimes a good game experience can be introduced into unusual settings. Consider the case of the "dreary conference" (see the Case in Point: Bringing Excitement to a Dreary Conference: The Bingo Hunt).

Step 2: Create Your Training Plan

Based on your module or course unit objectives, now analyze and list the tasks and topics you wish to cover in the lesson plan. First of all, list the tasks that relate to each module or course objective. One of your module or unit objectives might be to get participants to explain how they would manage all of the potential safety hazards within the workplace. Your list would look something like this:

Module Objective for Safety Training: Participants will be able to explain how they would manage all of the safety hazards within the workplace.

— List the potential hazards.
— Provide emergency plan instructions.
— Describe how to avoid or eliminate potential hazards.

From this list develop a flow of tasks and topics that coincide with the course/curriculum outcome. This flow is a draft of your lesson plan. Now you're ready for the next step—selecting and placing the training game in your lesson plan.

Case in Point

Bringing Excitement to a Dreary Conference: The Bingo Hunt

It was almost time for the Engineer's Annual Conference, a dreary three-day event filled with tired lecture-and-learn symposiums. Although the scientific updates were vital, the event was a double-pronged nightmare: First, administration had to convince engineers to set aside their busy schedule to attend, and second, it was becoming more difficult to locate experts willing and able to deliver credible training.

Suzanne, the new training specialist, was tasked with livening up the conference. After two weeks of interviews with previous instructors and attendees, she presented her plan—a daily luncheon activity that would require participants to use their lecture information to solve clues. The committee was dubious, pointing out that engineers "never played games." But after much discussion, and perhaps out of desperation, the committee gave Suzanne the go-ahead.

Preparation: Suzanne asked each presenter to submit the three most important facts in her or his presentation. From this collection of details, she prepared several short clues concerning each presentation or lecturer. When she had developed a total of 25 clues, Suzanne placed the clues into the squares of her 5 x 5 bingo-style game sheet.

Day 1: Engineers arrived at their luncheon tables to find a Bingo Hunt game sheet containing 25 clues that related to the morning lectures and presenters. Suzanne briefly went over the rules, explaining that the team (identified as all the people at any one table) who solved the most clues on the Bingo Hunt sheet would receive "valuable" prizes. Intrigued by the game sheet—or perhaps the prize list—people at each table immediately began matching the clues to the morning's sessions. When Suzanne called time, seven of the 12 table-teams had submitted their game sheets, and the time submitted was noted on each one. She tallied the sheets and awarded prizes to the team who had solved the most clues.

Day 2: There was a long queue of engineers waiting to enter the luncheon hall—and ready to play another round! Before they even ate, the men and women at each table met around the game sheets, sharing information about the presentations of the previous afternoon and that morning. With a wise eye to the clock, they rushed their lists to Suzanne. Again, time was called, the lists were reviewed, and prizes were awarded to the team with the most solved clues.

Day 3: The Bingo Hunt game sheets were hot items. Conference feedback forms indicated not only that Bingo Hunt was the favorite activity but that attendance was higher at each lecture after the first day's lunch.

For all the information you need to prepare, play, and debrief Bingo Hunt, see chapter 8.

Step 3: Select a Game for Your Training Plan

Establish a short list of expectations for what you want your training game to bring to your training plan. Your training game should deliver one or more of these criteria:

- review major learning points
- demonstrate the learner's level of topic understanding
- establish a baseline of how much the learner comprehends
- challenge the participants intellectually
- create an opportunity to demonstrate or practice skills.

When you have your criteria set out, you can select a game that will meet your expectations.

Step 4: Place the Game in the Lesson Plan

Here are eight places where games will work in an all-day training session:

1. as a starter activity to create a "comfortable" zone where interactivity is welcomed, even encouraged
2. just before morning break, to summarize main learning points
3. just after morning break, to review the morning module and segue into new content
4. just before lunch, again to summarize main learning points
5. just after lunch, to reenergize your audience, review the main learning points from the morning sessions, and segue into new content
6. just before afternoon break, to summarize main learning points
7. just following the afternoon break, to review the topic and focus on the final learning of the day
8. just before the day's session ends, to summarize learning.

Case in Point

Quiz Challenge and the Veteran Foremen

Corporation X's safety training required all learners to take a post-class certification exam to demonstrate their understanding of seven key safety factors. Here's the story of a trainer who simply compiled these facts into a quiz, added a challenge, and created a great "bait-for-freight" game.

It was time for the annual fire-safety review. This year the three-hour training was to be co-conducted by a veteran trainer assisting a fire-safety engineering graduate from the local university. Although the engineer was knowledgeable, she was shy and especially cautious about dealing with plant foremen twice her age.

The trainer decided on a challenge-and-response game that leveraged a challenge against a set of learning outcomes in the form of questions.

On class day the trainer first asked the foremen how many of the seven fire-safety questions they would answer correctly. From every man the defiant answer came: "Seven!" The number 7 was written on the chalkboard and the quizzes were handed out. After 10 minutes of anguished test taking, time was called. The trainer asked if anyone wanted to change his estimate. Suddenly repentant, the foremen downgraded their estimates to four, three, even two.

The training then was turned over to the engineer who confidently reviewed each and every response. At that point the foremen were interested in both the correctness of and the rationale behind every answer.

This simple game engaged the foremen and involved them in the topic. Fire-safety training became quite a popular topic, and class after class of foremen took the challenge quite seriously. Most important, they were very attentive during the mini-presentations that accompanied each correct answer.

Step 5: Consider Costs and Benefits

Each game should be assessed in terms of what it adds to the presentation and what it costs. To speak only of "benefits" ignores the costs of time, money, and resources; to mention only "costs" ignores the benefits of impact, interaction, and performance. The balance of these two factors and the acceptable trade-offs vary from trainer to trainer, and from training staff to training staff:

◈ Trainer A is willing to expend additional time in preparing a game to prompt real-time behavior and to heighten topic interest.

◈ Trainer B is willing to extend her budget to purchase a game that will increase the interaction between her players and the topic.

◈ Trainer C is willing to spend additional time locating game supplies and arranging the classroom to bring real-time application to the learning experience.

Case in Point

Learner, Come Back to Me

The workshop seemed blessed—it had good attendance and participants seemed genuinely interested in the topic. But the workshop was being held on-site and that caused widespread distractions, including numerous cases of participants returning late from breaks and meals. The trainers had a decision point—to restart class half full or extend each break by 15 minutes and lose valuable class time.

On the second day the trainers began awarding prizes. The "return-from-break" bell would be followed by the drawing of a participant's name from a bowl, and the winner would receive a key ring, coffee mug, or baseball cap. There was only one rule—you had to be present to win. Sure enough, soon the chairs were filled five minutes before breaks ended.

Use the cost-versus-benefits information presented in Chart 1-1 as an ongoing reminder of both the costs *and* benefits of introducing a learning game into your training.

Chart 1-1: The costs and benefits of games in your training.

Costs	Benefits
Preparation Time • Topic materials • Game materials • Game setup/cleanup	**Impact** • Heightened interest • Focus on topic • Real-time behaviors
Money • Purchase costs • User/rental fees • Special equipment fees	**Interaction** • Among individual players and teams of players • Between players and topic • Between players and rules and roles of team play
Resources • Game supplies/accessories • Facilities/storage/audiovisual equipment	**Performance** • Demonstration of content • Real-time application

A Checklist to Summarize What We've Covered

To serve as a type of summary to what we've covered in this chapter, Checklist 1-1 gives you a handy list of questions you should address before developing and using any training game. The checklist reminds you of specific issues and requirements you must address before you commit energy and resources to your learning experience.

Checklist I-I: Ten questions to ask and answer before using a training game.

1. Why do I want to use a game?
   - ☐ Specific learner payoffs:
     - increased involvement/motivation
     - greater interest
   - ☐ Specific instructor payoffs:
     - learner interaction with content
     - learner application of content

2. How will I link the learning to the overall curriculum?
   - ☐ Preview/review major learning points
   - ☐ Practice/apply concepts or principles

3. What do I expect will happen?
   - ☐ To learner—involvement, motivation, interest
   - ☐ To the content—demonstration of understanding, application of lessons learned

4. What is the monetary cost of the game?
   - $ _____ In direct outlay of purchase, rental, and/or licensing
   - $ _____ In indirect outlay for supplies, material, and equipment

5. What is/are the purpose(s) of the learning game?
   - ☐ Introduction, familiarity with topic
   - ☐ Demonstration of key learning points
   - ☐ Application of key skills or concepts

6. How much time do I need to . . .
   - ☐ Prepare the content material?
   - ☐ Prepare the game materials?
   - ☐ Prepare the visual aids and training room?
   - ☐ Set up and play the game?

7. Where will I use the game in my lesson plan?
   - ☐ To fit in a specific time slot
   - ☐ To focus on a specific topic or concept

8. What type of game do I want to use?
   - ☐ Reinforcement
   - ☐ Application
   - ☐ Team learning

9. Who is going to . . .
   Run the game? _____
   Debrief the game? _____

10. How will the game be debriefed?
    - ☐ With a focus on content
    - ☐ With a focus on behavior

The Beginning: Selecting Your Training Game

The beginning is the most important part of the work.

—Plato

The game development process begins with the selection of a training game. In this chapter we'll discuss criteria of a great training game. These criteria have been developed from a 10-year informal survey of game developers and facilitators who were asked, "What's the most important characteristic of an excellent training game?"

These are the three characteristics most often cited:

- **Game Appeal**—quality in the play and appearance of a game
- **Balanced Play**—the mix of game play and content
- **Flexibility**—adaptability of the game to your content and audience.

Game Appeal

When you're selecting a game, the first question to ask yourself is, "Would **I** want to play?" Think about it—would you want to participate in the play of this game? If your answer is "no," then you may want to revisit your game selection. After all, if you don't want to play the game, how will you ever be able to sell it to your learners? If you truly do enjoy the game, then your enthusiasm will be reflected in how well you develop content and materials for it.

A good game experience delivers a comfortable, at-play learning environment in which learners cheerfully transform into active, focused players. A good game experience should be

* visually appealing
* user friendly
* fun.

Visual Appeal

The chef's mantra—a food's visual presentation accounts for one-third of the taste experience—also applies to games. First, is the game itself appealing—the color and design of the game sheets, game boards, accessories, and packaging? Does the game "visually" invite play? Second, does the game invite play by offering an eye-catching and upbeat environment and room layout (walls, floor, tables, seating, even music and other sounds)? Does it stimulate several senses? Thoughtful use of posters, "designer" game sheets, and table layouts can pique participant interest before the game begins.

User-Friendliness

The game should be easy to introduce and play. The distribution of materials, explanation of the rules of play, and the start of game play should take 10 minutes or less. Instant recognition and a "ready-to-play" attitude could explain why many learning games are patterned after familiar parlor games, such as bingo, Jeopardy, Family Feud, and Monopoly.

Case in Point

Ms. Bonnie: The Metamorphosis

The university instructor was intrigued by the student who sat front-row/center. Ms. Bonnie scored well on exams but never smiled or reacted to lecture. Her preference was to observe all with a straight-ahead, emotionless stare. You could say that Ms. Bonnie was the classic night-class student, enduring the lecture in pursuit of a degree.

One night the instructor introduced a game. As students formed teams and game play began, a strange metamorphosis took place—students shook off indifference and came to life. Students once passive were now transformed into active players who noisily participated in the question-and-answer process. Even Ms. Bonnie showed signs of life as she prodded her team to near-victory.

When the game ended and the students returned to their seats, the instructor reviewed the content for a suddenly energized group. They were interested in not only what answers were the correct answers, but also why these answers were preferred. Even Ms. Bonnie raised her hand and participated in the follow-up lecture.

On future nights, when Ms. Bonnie returned to her natural state of indifference, the instructor fondly remembered that on the night of the game Ms. Bonnie was alive!

The Wise Trainer

Review Bingo, the once "perfect" game, just wasn't working, and the complaints varied from class to class. One group of participants claimed the game was no more than a game of chance; another class complained that the game was only a test—and a boring test at that.

   Informed of the complaints, the senior trainer wasn't surprised. She reminded her staff that as audiences varied in experience and education levels, so must the game's content. And the same was true of how the game was played.

The trainers reviewed the game play—rules, time allowed for question response, number of players on a team—as well as the topic questions. They made these changes: for professional groups, more short-answer questions, fewer players assigned to each team, and shorter question periods; for service personnel, more multiple-choice questions, expanded team membership, and greater time for questions and answers.

   With the dual emphasis on both lesson *and* game development, it only took three sessions to make Review Bingo the "perfect" game again.

Fun

Game play should create a buoyant, smiling learning zone—a nonthreatening place where it's fun to participate and learn. Game play should be a way to celebrate your content, demonstrated by smiling learners who enthusiastically interact with the content.

Balance: The Mix of Game Play and Content

The recipe for balanced play is a dash of well-prepared content mixed with the action of the game, and thoughtfully served to your audience. Well-balanced play is that most unique of learning experiences in which game play drives interest in the topic while the topic drives interest in the game. Where else but in a learning game would players anxiously await the next topic question in their effort to fulfill a game requirement?

   Keeping a game in balance is a series of continuous adjustments:

   ◆ If a game is front-loaded with too much play—more chance than challenge—then adjustments must be made, such as slowing down game play or adding more content.

   ◆ If a game is end-loaded with content, which makes it a not-so-cleverly-disguised test, then adjustments must be made, such as adding more risk or revising the level of content.

Flexibility: Adapting the Game Frame to Your Content and Audience

Does the game fit or can it be adapted to your content and audience? Even if the game is appealing and shows balance between content and play, what good is it if it doesn't adapt to your material? Games that are adaptable are usually called "frames" or templates. An "open frame" accepts almost any material and can be adapted to any level of use—learning level, audience size, and number of players, to mention three.

A good example of an open frame game is the familiar tic-tac-toe template.

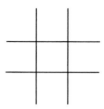

Remember how we made this a training game by requiring players to "earn" spaces with correct answers? Start-up requires pairing participants in opponent-dyads and then quickly "loading the frame," or inserting your content questions into the play of the game. Here's how it goes:

- *Round 1:* Player "X" selects a space.
- Facilitator presents question 1.
- Player "X" gives response to opponent.
  - If correct, Player "X" covers the space.
  - If incorrect, the space remains clear.
- Play alternates to Player "O" and the same rules apply.

Game flexibility refers to the games' adaptability in the following five areas: content, learning level, number of players, available resources, and time requirements. Let's look more closely at each area:

1. **Content.** The frame should accept almost any content, from hazardous materials to vocabulary review. You should be able to directly insert content in the form of questions or very short scenarios into the flow of the game. For the Tic-Tac-Topic training game, this requires developing 10 content questions that are presented on a round-by-round basis during play.

    In addition, the game should fit the content flow of your lesson plan. In other words, the game can be used to

    — introduce a topic

    — review the topic

    — complement the lecture

    — require application of the topic through problem solving

    — serve miscellaneous purposes, such as refocus the class when everyone returns from a break.

Case in Point

Don't Call It a Game!

As the training staff struggled to meet the latest crunch deadline, the junior staff member suggested using a training game to review the half-day seminar. The response from senior staff members was immediate: "This is *important* training; we don't use games! Training is serious business here at ABC Company!"

But, because all company training required baseline justification—verification that the learners understood the training—the junior member got his chance by volunteering to conduct a post-course "review" consisting of a 10-question short-answer quiz addressing the key learning points.

At the end of the class, "Junior" handed out the quiz to each participant. He asked everyone to complete the "review" individually and then meet with the rest of their tablemates and select their one best set of responses. At the end of 10 minutes, Junior collected one quiz sheet from each table and read each question aloud, along with the correct response. Then he gave each participant a candy bar and thanked them for their efforts.

Perhaps it was the candy bar or the friendly competition prompted by the quiz, but "review" time became the anticipated closure to a seminar. The event was even expanded to include an awards ceremony where the traditional candy bar was augmented with prizes awarded to the tablemates with the best score.

The game that wasn't a "game" was the start of what is now the traditional review ceremony.

Trainer's Tip:
Identify a "game" as an "activity" or an "exercise"—anything that seems to add gravitas.

2. **Learning Level.** The frame should adapt to almost any learner's education and experience levels. This usually requires that the questions be written to suit the appropriate level:

— educational level (eighth grade to graduate student)

— professional level (service worker to executive)

— work experience (first year on the job to long-time employee)

— life experience (student, military, rural, inner-city, elder, among others)

— language skills (basic reading and writing, English as a second language, technical vocabulary).

3. **Number of Players.** The frame should be playable (with the appropriate adaptations listed in Tool 2-1: Group Size Adaptation Chart) with groups of almost any number of members:

— small (four to 8 players)

— medium (nine to 18 players)

— large (19 to 36 players)

— very large (36 or more players).

4. **Available Resources.** The game should use readily available office resources, such as pencils, paper, index cards, felt-tipped markers, and masking tape. It should be

Tool 2-1: Group Size Adaptation Chart

	Small Group (4-8)	Medium Group (9-18)	Large Group (19-36)	X-Large Group (37-100)
Time for...				
Introduction	Normal/shortened	Normal	Extra time may be needed	Extra time needed
Game Play	Normal/expanded	Normal	Extra time may be needed	Extra time needed
Rounds of Play	Normal/expanded	Normal	Normal rounds—expand time Normal time—fewer rounds	Normal rounds—expand time Normal time—fewer rounds
Debriefing	Normal/expanded	Normal	Normal debriefing—expand time Less debriefing—normal time	Normal debriefing—expand time Less debriefing—normal time
Team				
Player Roles	Assign extra roles to each player	Regular assignments	Players may have to share roles	Players share roles or limit number of teams
Teams/Size	One team, small to average size	Two or more teams of average size	Four or more teams of average size	Eight or more teams of average size
Interteam Play	No, in most cases	Yes	Yes, time is limited	Yes; time and play are limited
Content				
Amount	Normal/expanded	Normal	Normal/less content	Less content
Level	Normal/accelerated	Normal	Normal/less demanding	Normal/less demanding
Administration				
Room size	Smaller/normal	Normal	Larger facilities	Much larger facilities
Setup	Less/normal	Normal	Extra materials and prior setup may be required	Extra materials and prior setup required
Audiovisual	Less/normal	Normal	Additional audiovisual equipment and setup	Additional audiovisual equipment and setup
Tracking game play	Easy	Normal	Difficult; may require additional monitors	Very difficult; requires additional monitors
Observation	Easy	Normal	Difficult; may require additional observers	Very difficult; requires additional observers

playable in ordinary training settings, such as at tables, writing desks, or one-armed chairs. It should require only basic audiovisual equipment, such as flipcharts and easels, overhead projectors, chalkboards/whiteboards, and PowerPoint presentations. The game accessories should be available or accessible, such as chips; dice; Koosh balls; pawns (tokens); and ordinary household items, such as a soup bowl and plate.

5. **Time Requirements.** The game should be flexible enough to fit into a specific timed segment of your lesson timeline. This flexibility enables you to use the game in one or all of these time slots:

— at the start to kick off the topic or lecture

— just before lunch or morning/afternoon break

— just after lunch or morning/afternoon break

— at day's end as a "closer" or summary event.

CHAPTER 3

Preparations: The Game Plan

Begin with the end in mind.

—Stephen Covey

After a thoughtful search, you have selected your training game and now look toward preparation—those steps that help you choose the material you'll present in the game format and the tasks that transform your material into a game activity. It's here that a plan of action is needed. To that end, we offer you a step-by-step checklist appropriately named the "Game Plan" (see Tool 3-1).

Overall, its purpose is to help you

- identify what materials and resources you will need
- stay on track in the development of the game
- sequence your game activity
- conduct and debrief the game
- maintain a written record for future use.

The Game Plan checklist takes you from game selection to game closure and debriefing. Now let's look more closely at some of the individual elements of this plan.

Title of the Game

Game Plan: Working Checklist

Title: _____

Tool 3-1: Game Plan: Working Checklist

Title: _____

Format: _____

Overview:

   Purpose: _____

   Use: _____

   Audience: _____

   Number of Players: _____

   Time Needed to Play Game: _____

Game Materials/Props: _____

_____

_____

Equipment: _____

_____

_____

Room Setup: _____

_____

_____

Before Game Play:

_____

_____

_____

_____

_____

How to Play the Game:

_____

_____

_____

_____

_____

_____

After Game Play—Debriefing:

_____

_____

_____

_____

_____

_____

The first step in using the Game Plan is to select a game whose format and pattern of play suit your content, your audience, and your personal taste. For the sake of example, we'll choose the favorite learning game of the Practice of Management class at the University of Maryland. It's a two-part learning game with a question-and-answer quiz followed by a target-throw activity. The game is called "Toss Up."

Audience

> **Game Plan: Working Checklist**
>
> **Title:** _____
>
> **Format:** _____
>
> **Overview:**
>   Purpose: _____
>   Use: _____
>   Audience: _____

The Game Plan prompts you to identify the audience you'll be training. It is the audience that determines the level to which you have to gear your content and the amount of time you'll need to cover it. Consider the experience and knowledge level of the audience. How much work and life experience will the audience be bringing to the training topic? Will the game be offered to a specific target population or a broader audience? Answering these questions will help you decide if you need content at a basic level or at a more advanced level. Most adults bring a broad base of experiences to learning, so think about how can you draw on that experience in the game activity.

For example, Toss Up could be aimed at first-line supervisors—those who may be familiar with the tasks of the job but need help in managing how they divide their time between the demands of the job and the needs of their direct reports.

Purpose

> **Game Plan: Working Checklist**
>
> **Title:** _____
>
> **Format:** _____
>
> **Overview:**
>   Purpose: _____

The element of the plan that focuses on describing the game's purpose is the first step in developing your learning game.

Any type of process often starts with the end product (its ultimate purpose) in mind. For instance, a house design often starts with the architect's full-color elevation drawings or a three-dimensional model complete with tiny people and toy cars. Approach this step in the same way: Begin by visualizing the final outcome to help you state your purpose, identify the tasks involved, and develop the material. With an eye to your goal, you're more likely to be able to hold your focus on the pieces needed to create that end product. The purpose is similar to an overall objective, goal, or terminal objective. In designing our training, we often set the end goal first, and then work backward in a systematic way. Like designing to the test, it ensures that we design our game and the game content to meet our training objectives.

In writing formal training objectives, you may have used Robert Mager's formula featuring these three criteria:

1. **Performance**—what do you want the participants to do?
2. **Conditions**—under what conditions will they do it?
3. **Acceptable Level**—at what standard do they need to perform?

For example, a training objective might look like this: "At the end of the team-building workshop, participants will be able to describe all 10 of the team behaviors, and provide an example of each." This objective would meet Mager's criteria in these ways: Participants **describe all 10 of the team behaviors** (*performance*) in a **team-building workshop** (*conditions*), and they do it **with 100 percent accuracy** (*acceptable level*).

Although not as formal as training objective statements, game purpose descriptions should relate to your training objectives and help define your workshop content. Your game may have one or more of the following purposes:

- to review content
- to introduce a topic
- to introduce an activity
- to apply a concept or a theory
- to apply a skill
- to improve skills
- to demonstrate learning
- to provide feedback to learner and trainer.

Sample game purpose statements built on those objectives would look like this:

- to demonstrate learning of the topic
- to demonstrate increased skill

- to create a team learning experience
- to review major learning points
- to experience risk.

Identifying Content

The next step in developing the game is to determine what information needs to be presented so that participants will be able to complete the game successfully. At this point you are breaking your content down into pieces, listing what information is needed so that participants will complete the game purpose—that is, will meet your ultimate objective for the game.

Your material breakdown would look something like this:

- **Game Purpose**—Explain the 10 team behaviors
- **Content Breakdown**—Topic: task and maintenance behaviors
- **Five Task Behaviors**
  1. Initiating
     a. Gets a conversation going
     b. Proposes tasks
  2. Information or opinion seeking
     a. Draws out opinions, ideas, beliefs
  3. Information or opinion giving
     a. Shares opinions, ideas, beliefs
  4. Clarifying
     a. Rephrases statements
     b. Clears up confusion
  5. Summarizing
     a. Pulls ideas together
     b. Offers conclusions.
- **Five Maintenance Behaviors**
  1. Encouraging
     a. Responds to others in a positive way
     b. Uses eye contact
  2. Offering acceptance
     a. Approves others' participation, verbally or nonverbally
  3. Harmonizing/compromising
     a. Manages disagreements
     b. Reduces tensions
  4. Gatekeeping
     a. Helps others contribute
     b. Encourages non-participants to be involved

5. Sharing feelings
   a. Sharing feelings with the group, and getting others to express their feelings.

At this point, you have listed your topic, your main points (headings), and the key information that is needed so that participants can complete the game purpose. You will keep filling in the required information and drilling down further into the content detail.

If you're not familiar with the details of the content, you may want to consult a subject-matter expert (SME) who can give you more specific information. This helps ensure that you're on track in developing your game content, and that you're including the key information that is needed.

Although an SME may find it tempting to include everything that is known on a particular topic, if you focus on "need to know," instead of "nice to know," your learners will be able to perform and retain at a higher level. Most of the time, players pick up the "nice to know" while involved with the "need to know" portion of the information. Your role is to get the participants to be able to perform the game purpose successfully.

Resources for Developing Content

To help you gather content for your game, in addition to your own subject matter knowledge, you can consult these resources:

- trade journals/publications
- other SMEs
- practitioners
- other trainers
- Websites
- books
- DVDs, videos, audiotapes.

Trainer's Tip:

Develop 25 percent more question items than you think you'll use, keeping the extra questions to replace questions on the spot or for use in additional rounds of play.

Developing Game Questions

Questions are the heart of your learning game experience. They bring individual content items to the direct attention of your audience in a series of unique, stop-and-focus learning moments. And by sequencing these moments you create a comfortable flow for your content.

In the previous section, we discussed breaking down the information that participants will need if they are to fulfill the game purpose successfully. We now turn our attention to creating question items. Appropriately written and positioned questions add to both the learning and the fun of your game. This section will cover some techniques and tips for writing insightful questions.

Three Question-Development Techniques

Technique 1: Create a Test

The most direct way to develop questions is to write a test on your topic, focusing on the key learning points or "need to know" information items. Develop 30 or so test items that address your major learning points, making sure each item "stands alone" (that is, it addresses only one point or concept). If needed, create a batch of two to four questions to cover different aspects of the same concept.

Technique 2: Triage Your Questions

After you have created your question items, go through them to

- prioritize from most vital to least vital
- sequence the placement of your questions to decide which questions
  - appear early, in the middle of, or late in game play
  - precede or follow other questions to introduce or wrap up a concept or application
- identify which questions should receive special treatment or observation— questions that create their own dialogue may distract from game play, but this could add to classroom learning
- eliminate questions that might prove vague or confusing.

During the question-sorting process, you may find it easier to place each question on a separate index card. The index-sort saves time, avoids the confusion of multiple checklists and cross-offs, and yields an immediate game product (a stack of question cards). When the final sorting process is complete, place the questions in the appropriate order on the game sheets, question cards, PowerPoint slides, or overhead transparencies.

Technique 3: Zoom In, Zoom Out

This technique takes a wide-angle view, then a tight-in view. It visualizes the whole game as a tapestry or "big picture"; zooms in to position one or more questions on a learning point; then zooms out to see how this placement fits in with the whole game concept. Continue zooming in (question placement) and zooming out (stepping back to see how it all fits) until you have filled the game with your question items. This technique helps create a balanced and focused game presentation.

Tips for Developing Questions

Questions are your way to customize the game to your topic and learners. Think of each question as your opportunity to focus on a particular learning point. When you review the correct response, you can add to the learning moment—the time immediately after

Trainer's Tip:

To create a stack of question cards, batch eight questions per sheet of paper—two columns, four questions to a column— and then cut each sheet into eight mini-sheets. Use these mini-sheets for your index sort or for question cards when playing the Card Sort game (see chapter 8 for details on that game).

Trainer's Tip:

The zoom-in/zoom-out technique can be created by teaming two developers and having each of them select their preferred "in" or "out" function. By adopting opposing perspectives, each drives the other—zoom in to specific questions (focus), zoom out to the entire presentation (balance).

the presentation of a correct response—to include information that provides the rationale (why a response is correct or incorrect) and that elaborates (underscores) the importance and expands the meaning of the correct response. The following tips should help you prepare your questions:

- **Focus each question on one fact.** This keeps the information precise and brief, and makes it easier to prioritize and sequence the question flow. If needed, use several questions to ensure that the learning concept is adequately covered.

- **Write questions in a conversational format.** This adds to the informality of play and, because many questions are read aloud, helps the flow of the game.

- **Be brief and use simple wording for both questions and answers.** As a rule, questions should contain fewer than 25 words, especially if read aloud.

- **Use numbering.** Number and date each question for review and updating. This helps you track your questions and then replace, in-kind, any question that is outdated or needs revision. Simply refer to your question list (or stack of cards), and replace the outdated question with the updated one (also numbered and dated). Numbering your questions also enables you to note and track question(s) that seemed particularly difficult or incomprehensible to your class and then replace as necessary.

Creating a Question Mix

Games allow you to mix your question items in a variety of ways. Here are two of those ways:

1. **Preview-to-Review Mix.** Games are an excellent way to introduce new material and review content you've already covered or that learners already know. Given the randomness of play, even if the question item concerns new material, it's considered just "part of the game." When a preview question allows for intelligent guessing—by use of multiple-choice options or hints built into the question— then the player (team) always has a chance to provide a correct response—with the added bonus of the complete focus of *all* players, both responders and nonanswering opponents alike, when the correct response, along with supporting rationale, is given during the answer period.

   — **3-to-1 Rule:** To introduce new question material, mix the new (or preview) questions with review (material already covered) in a 3-to-1 ratio; three questions that review material already covered for every one question that previews upcoming material. This both creates a good question mix and piques player interest in the new topic.

2. **Difficulty Mix.** Many game facilitators like to create a user-friendly climate by starting the game with simpler questions. This lets players get a sense of what information is required of them while they get used to the rules and roles of game play. After two or three questions you can increase the difficulty of the material. Lots of trainers like to position the more difficult, and meaningful, questions toward the end of game play, knowing that player application of that material is more vital.

— **1-3-1 Rule:** To create a difficulty mix for your question batch, develop a 1-3-1 difficulty ratio for every five question items—one easy, three moderately challenging, and one difficult. This mix is not seen as threatening, but rather as a part of game play that varies the rhythm and keeps it interesting.

— **Up-Down Technique:** Create a difficulty mix by writing your questions "up" or "down"—that is, create "levels" of difficulty by simply using different question types.

  • **Develop-Down:** To make a difficult question item easier, write it in a multiple-choice or true-false format. For example, the question, "Name the consumer protest technique that businesspeople hate most," could be restated "down" as, "Which of these three consumer protest techniques do businesspeople hate most—boycott, picketing, or letters of complaint?" The direct question requires the player to know, or at best guess at, the correct response. The multiple-choice allows the player to see the field of correct responses and select the most appropriate one.

  • **Develop-Up:** To write a question "up," use a reverse modification, such as changing "Are the tissues of the body that are most susceptible to damage due to decreased blood supply located in the (a) heart, (b) lungs, or (c) brain?" to this direct question: "Where in the body are the tissues most susceptible to damage due to decreased blood supply?"

Sample Question Types

Facilitators and instructors are proficient question writers. It's our way to challenge, test, and review information. The following sample question formats are meant to guide you in the different ways to place your content in the game.

  ❖ **Direct question:** This question type requires players to identify a person, place, or thing. Be sure to include enough information to enable players to provide the proper answer.

  Q: Name the consumer protest technique that businesspeople hate the most.
  A: Picketing.

◆ **Fill-in-the-blank:** This question type requires the player to identify the information needed in the blank space. This format is simpler to answer than the direct question because you specify what is expected in the blank space or because the position
of the space gives a hint.

Q: Service sector jobs now make up more than ___ percent of all U.S. employment.
A: 74 percent. (Accept 70 to 80 percent.)

◆ **Multiple-choice:** This question type presents the correct response along with two distracting responses. This format can make a difficult item easier by presenting the player with choices. Questions should offer no more
than three choices; four (or more) choices can be confusing and will
slow down play.

Q: Are the tissues of the body most susceptible to damage due to decreased blood supply located in the (a) heart, (b) lungs, or (c) brain?
A: (c) Brain

◆ **True or false:** This is the easiest type of question to prepare and answer, and it offers players a 50/50 chance to respond correctly. The format can help players ease into competition. Limit this format to fewer than 20 percent of all the game questions to keep the game from becoming a "flip of the coin" exercise.

Q: Married people enjoy better health than single people. True or False?
A: True.

◆ **Partial listing:** Players must identify multiple items from a list of correct responses. Ask for a few, but not all, of the items on the list to reduce frustration of total recall. The complete list should be read when the answer is reviewed with the class.

Q: Name two of the three primary colors.
A: Accept any two of red, blue, and yellow.

◆ **Computation:** This format requires the player quickly to compute a mathematical, accounting, or logical sequencing process. It can be used to introduce or reinforce data essential to the topic.

Q: A $125.00 coat is on sale at a 40 percent discount. What is the price of the coat?
A: $75.00.

◆ **Demonstration:** This requires the player to perform a particular skill or task. The instructor can use the time during validation to quickly remind learners of the appropriate procedures used to complete the task correctly.

Q: Demonstrate the correct procedure used in taking a radial pulse.
A: Place forefinger over the radial artery (inside of wrist), count the pulse for 15 (or 30) seconds, and then multiply by 4 (or 2, respectively).

Trainer's Tip:

When given an oral response, be sure to restate the complete response during the validation or correct response portion of the question. This reinforcement encourages greater understanding, internalization, and application of the information.

❖ **Case study:** This requires the player to analyze and discuss learning points presented in a written description of a problem, and then to analyze and recommend a solution or solutions to solve the problem.

Guidelines for developing your scenario:

— Write in story form—create a short word picture.

— Develop characters—create a mini-situation focusing on one or two characters.

— Provide details—the case study should contain enough information to create a problem situation that must be addressed or resolved. In the Quinn Electronics example (see below), the case study should provide enough details about the manager's itinerary and priorities, and should challenge your participants' scheduling skills.

— Provide tasks or questions—specify what you expect of your participants, the questions to be answered or the tasks to be performed.

A simple time management case study with player instructions might start like this:

You work at Quinn Electronics. It's Tuesday afternoon and you're planning your next workday. You have several important tasks waiting for your attention, including a series of morning meetings all week. Your "A" priority is the Stone Quarry Project, due on your boss's desk Friday morning at 10. Here's a list of your appointments and workload:... [a list of priority projects]. Your task is to prepare your "To Do Lists" for Wednesday and Thursday.

Time Needed to Play the Game

Game Plan: Working Checklist

Title: _____

Format: _____

Overview:
   Purpose: _____
   Use: _____
   Audience: _____
   Number of Players: _____
   Time Needed to Play Game: _____

This is the position on the Game Plan Checklist where you establish timelines. You decide how much time is needed to present and cover your game's content (question items). Base your decision on the amount of content, the level or complexity, and where the game is going to be placed in the lesson plan.

Let's return to our original game example, Toss Up. Recall that we identified our audience as first-line supervisors. In our effort to develop material, we created 30 question items, and here's how they've been sorted:

- Need to know, important or crucial information—13 question items
- Nice to know, helpful, but not vital—14 items
- Supplemental information, marginally helpful, and good for extended play or tie-breakers—3 items.

To compute the **time** needed for play, review the time requirements of the intended game (Toss Up), as follows:

- identify the number of information items (13 "need to know" plus 2 "nice to know")
- check the lesson plan for available time (one hour)
- estimate the amount of time that playing the game will require (each round takes 15-20 minutes to play—five questions per round for three rounds of play).

Finally, establish a **question sequence.** For this game we set the sequence from the most basic material (round 1), to intermediate material (round 2), to the most complex material (round 3).

◈

In this chapter we've presented a step-by-step process that guides you in the development of the question content, the heart of your training game experience. Chapter 4 will review the four low-tech game formats that are easy to adapt and have a proven track record of successful play—namely, manual (paper-and-pencil) games, card games, board games, and prop games. Chapter 5 then uses one of the games, Toss Up, in a step-by-step guide to the preparations you need to make so you can introduce and play your training game.

Training Game Formats

Always know your props.

—Buster Keaton

Game Plan: Working Checklist

Title: _____

Format: _____

 game's format is what is required in terms of materials and mechanics of play. In this book our focus is on "low-tech" games—games that

- do not depend on electronic equipment for presentation
- can be created with materials found in most offices and homes.

There are four basic low-tech training game formats:

1. manual games
2. card games
3. board games
4. prop games.

Training games usually are one or a combination of these four formats.

Manual Games

These games are played with paper and pencil, and may use game or play sheets, puzzles, case studies, problems, and scenarios. Most manual games can be produced with desktop publishing software, inkjet or laser printers, and copying machines.

The game's most obvious advantages are in their economy and the control of production. Because manual games rely on ordinary paper supplies, they can be produced easily, allowing you to produce only as many game sheets as you need. You can customize the game sheets with your specific topic information and corporate logo. And players appreciate the take-home reference notes that manual game sheets provide.

Examples of manual games include bingo, tic-tac-toe, quiz games, and instructional puzzles.

The Eight-Sentence Rule

It's easier for players to adjust to game play when the rules are simple and straightforward. This enables them to focus attention on content rather than be preoccupied with a series of rules. The eight-sentence rule operates in two ways:

1. Stating all the rules of the game in eight sentences or fewer avoids confusion and creates immediate play.

2. Keeping the rules to no more than eight sentences restrains you from adding details or options to address situations that may never arise during game play. If a situation arises that requires extra instruction or rule adjustment while the game is being played, it can be addressed at that time. For example, in Board Bingo a player only needs to reroll the die when all matching game board numbers are covered—let's say the player rolls a "4" and all "4" spaces are occupied by a chip. This adjustment, the rerolling of the die, may happen 15 to 20 minutes into game play, if it happens at all. To explain this possibility at the beginning takes away from the immediate play of the game and adds a layer of complexity that isn't needed.

Trainer's Tip:
Ordinary playing cards may not be accepted by certain religious groups who associate cards with gambling. Players with objections can be removed from direct play, but asked to observe and report on important aspects of the game.

Sample Game: Review Bingo

To prepare for a game of Review Bingo, the trainer selects 25 key learning points from the text or handout material. These learning points are the basis for the "review." The trainer then creates a set of 25 clues that prompt the player to search the material to find the missing information. Finally, the trainer places the 25 answers on a 5 x 5 bingo-style game sheet and produces one sheet for every two players. (You'll find detailed instructions for this game in chapter 8.) For this sample game, we've created the game sheet in Figure 4-1.

**Figure 4-1. Sample Review Bingo game sheet:
Introduction to management.**

Gilbreth	McGregor	Synergy	Hawthorn Studies	FW Taylor
Gen X	Weber	Maslow	Systems Theory	Follett
Parker-Follett	Hawthorne Effect	Gantt	Closed System	Barnard
Contingency	Theory Y	TQM	Fayol	Theory X
Blake and Mouton	Gen Y	Open System	Theory Z	Feedback

Game Play

1. The trainer presents the first clue: "Name the Father of Scientific Management."
2. Each player puts a token on his or her selected square.
3. Instructor presents the correct response: "F.W. Taylor."
4. If the player has put a token on the correct square, he or she removes the token and draws an "X" through the square. If the selected square was not correct, the player simply removes the token. This completes one round of play.
5. Play is the same for all rounds, and continues until a player covers five spaces in a row and wins the game.

Card Games

These are games based on specially prepared cards or ordinary playing cards. Specially prepared cards, usually prepared by the trainer, can be played by themselves (such as

Trainer's Tip:

Printing Cards: The traditional card size is 2.75" x 4", or eight-to-a-sheet (U.S. letter). The eight-sheet is divided into two rows at four cards per sheet, and it's printed horizontally, or "landscape." Cut each sheet into eight individual cards and then collate into card sets for each player-group.

Shortcut: At an office supply store you can find packs of blank 2.5" x 3" cards, 10 to a sheet, ready to print on your office inkjet or laser printer and perforated for easy separation. Prepare clues of 15 words or less to fit on the cards, and lay them out using simple desktop publishing software. Then print, separate, and collate into stacks.

the Flashcards identification game) or be used as part of another game (for example, as question cards for a board game or a sorting exercise).

The advantages of a card game lie in its focus, simplicity, and portability:

- **Focus:** Each card focuses on a specific worksite issue or topic.
- **Simplicity:** Each card is self-contained and self-explanatory, and most people will be familiar with the general concept of a card game.
- **Portability:** Cards can be carried and stored easily.

Ordinary playing cards can be purchased in a variety of styles, including super-sized ones for group play and novelty decks that are sliced in half. Use cards to select team members randomly for team games. Examples include specialty card games such as Flashcards and the playing card game Barnga (see www.thiagi.com).

There are two disadvantages for specially prepared (customized) cards:

1. It can be expensive. Using customized cards requires printing one set of cards for each player-group or team, so printing question cards for six teams requires six (or more) sets of cards (20-40 cards per set) for game play. If you have a professional print shop or copy area, workers there may have some ideas that will address this resource problem.

2. Printed question cards usually have a shelf life of three years or less before some or all of the cards need to be updated or replaced.

Sample Game: Card Sort

Let's look at a card game example. We're going to use a card game to enable players to demonstrate their understanding of different categories, decision points, stages, or steps of a workflow process. We want our players to differentiate between two categories, demonstrating their understanding of simple mathematical operations. We first define the two categories ("odds" and "evens") and then develop 15 to 25 situations or "item cards." (*Developing* item cards can range from simply writing up a set of index cards—a different color card for each team—to printing the cards through your desktop publishing software or at your on-site print shop or copy area.)

Game Play

1. Divide the group into two or more teams.
2. Have each team line up single-file in front of a chart posted on the wall (see Figure 4-2).
3. Distribute one set of 24 item cards and a role of masking tape to each team.
4. With team members working in "relay style," give teams two minutes to place each card in the appropriate category.
5. The team that successfully sorts the most cards in two minutes wins.

Figure 4-2: Sample Card Sort setup.

Odds	Evens

Sample Card Problems [with answers]

$3 + 7 + (12–1) = [21 = odd]$

$2^3 \times 3 + 7 = [31 = odd]$

Square root of 16 + 2/3 of 9 =
[10 = even]

Board Games

These are games played on a specially designed surface or game board. Play on the game board usually requires the use of question cards, dice, pawns or markers, chips or play money, and other accessories. The use of game boards gets high ratings for prompting players' initial attraction, and very high marks for enhancing the quality of play.

Because board games enable you to dramatize specific discussions or topics on a card-by-card basis, they have produced some of the most memorable real-time experiences in indoor play. In a career- planning class, this ingeniously written game card seemed to sum up the entire focus of the workshop:

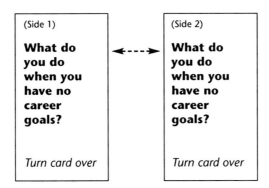

Imagine the player's "aha!" as he or she kept turning this card over and over!

Another instructor wanted to demonstrate the effect of how an inappropriate question could sabotage even the most positive interview experience. He created this card for his board game:

> Ask the player on your left this question:
>
> "Have you seen my wallet?"

The effect was immediate and powerful. This one question card prompted a meaningful post-game dialogue about intent versus effect in questioning techniques.

Creating a board game experience can be very expensive in terms of money and time. Game play usually requires one complete game set for four to eight players. A class of 24 could require three to six complete game sets, including boards; question cards; and accessories such as dice, chips, and play money.

There are three available supply sources you can consider when you're developing board games for your training sessions:

1. **Ready-to-Play Games** can be purchased off the shelf or you may commission a professional game developer to customize a game for your topic, audience, or event. Off-the-shelf game sets are available for generic topics, such as time management, leadership, or customer service. These pilot-tested games provide a good learning experience. You may want to review the question cards to ensure they are specific to your topic and audience, removing nonspecific or counterproductive item cards. Customized games are developed specially for your topic and audience. Outside development costs range upwards of $5,000 to create a set—that is, enough game boards and accessories for a class of 18 students.

2. **Frame Games** are ready-to-play game templates that you fill with your topic. You take a familiar game structure, such as bingo, and customize it by writing topic questions. Frame games can be labor intensive, often requiring production capabilities in making the question cards.

3. **Do-It-Yourself or In-House Games** are labor intensive and require you to create everything the game uses, including question cards, game boards, and accessories (dice, pawns, spinners, play money). Time and financial constraints may make this option the least desirable game source. But some thoughtful and exciting in-house games evolve into excellent training vehicles and fully justify the upfront investments. A board game we originally developed for a single use in a

Trainer's Tip:

Eliminate question cards by presenting each question on an overhead transparency or PowerPoint slide, and have the answering team present its response to the opposing team.

university leadership program quickly became a class favorite, and with one or two rule changes the game has been converted to a frame game that's open to any content. (The game is called Board Bingo and we offer it for your classroom use. See chapter 8 for details.)

Board Game Basics

The two most adaptable board game structures are "follow-the-path" and "qualify-and-score."

1. **Follow-the-Path.** Players advance along the game board by a mechanism (such as rolling dice) and/or by question-and-answer. Here are the two most-common formats:

   — The Monopoly format requires players to travel around a continuing game path and follow "rules of the space." Dice rolls advance the player's token, and correct responses earn points, chips, or other rewards, such as an extra turn. The winner is the player who has accumulated the most money or chips when time is called.

   — The Candyland format requires the winning player to complete the entire game path before any opponent does so. Dice rolls advance the player's token, and correct responses earn points or other rewards.

2. **Qualify-and-Score.** Made popular by Trivial Pursuit, this format asks players to "qualify" by answering a question or responding to a situation *before* they advance their tokens, occupy a space, or receive a reward.

Sample Game: Board Bingo

Board Bingo is a qualify-and-score board game in which players role a die, select a space that matches the number rolled, and then answer a question to earn the selected space.

Game Play

1. Divide the group into sets of teams, with two teams per game board. (See Figure 4-3 for a black-and-white version of the board game, or see the color version on the accompanying CD.)
2. Have each team select one die and chips of the same color.
3. Have Team A roll first and select a space that matches the number rolled.
4. Present the first question on an overhead transparency or PowerPoint slide and have Team A give its response to the opposing team.
5. Present the correct response on transparency or slide.
6. If Team A's response was correct, one of its chips is placed on the selected space. If it was incorrect, the turn is over and Team B rolls its die.
7. Play continues until one team gets five of its chips lined up in a row.

Figure 4-3. Sample Board Bingo game board.

1	4	5	3	2
2	5	3	1	4
3	2	4	5	1
4	3	1	2	5
5	1	2	4	3

Prop Games

This fourth type of manual game is played on or with one or more props, such as building blocks, specialty or regular dice, targets, ropes, wallcharts, or floor grids.

The greatest advantage of a prop game is in the player's action with the prop. Players get the hands-on experience of throwing the dice and darts, catching the Koosh ball, or crossing the floor grid.

Preparations require you to collect and store props, and it takes additional time to set up and dismantle the game. Wall games require that you prepare and post a chart. For floor games you must lay down grids or obstacles using masking tape, traffic cones, or props on a hard or carpeted floor.

Here are some examples of low-tech prop games (that are described in detail later in the book):

- ◆ **Wall Game**—Match Point, a forced-match creativity game, is played on a wallchart. Teams develop items suggested by the match of letters and categories on each square of the game sheet—for example, a new use for a cake mix, starting with "C," could be "cookies." Here's a sample wallchart (with answers filled in) for a game that focuses on brainstorming new uses for existing products:

	C	**S**	**W**
Cake mix	cookies	short-bread	waffles
Liquid soap	CD cleaner	stain remover	weather-proofing
Plastic bags	chair pockets	shoe storage	wash-and-store food bags

- **Floor Grid**—Sand Trap, a floor game, requires each team to determine a safe crossing path—avoiding the nine sand traps—and then send five players safely across the floor grid in less than a minute.
- **Target Game**—Toss Up uses a qualify-and-score mechanism. Players qualify by answering five questions, earning one throw for each correct response. They score points by tossing objects into a target space.

Sample Games: Sand Trap and Toss Up

Let's use Sand Trap and Toss Up as our prop game examples. (As with all the other examples in this chapter, these games will be described in detail in chapter 8.)

The floor grid for Sand Trap is a matrix of 25 numbered squares, each measuring about one foot. Nine squares in the grid contain "sand traps." The object is to safely cross the grid without entering a sand-trap space. Here's an illustration of the Sand Trap floor grid:

◄——— **FINISH LINE** ———►

21	22	23	24	25
16	17	18	19	20
11	12	13	14	15
6	7	8	9	10
1	2	3	4	5

◄——— **STARTING LINE** ———►

Sand Trap Game Play

1. Divide into teams of five or more players.
2. Tell teams they have 10 minutes to plan how to send five players safely across the floor grid.
3. Have each team select a set of clues.
4. After 10 minutes, have the first team line up at the starting line on the floor grid.
5. Give each team one minute for
   — the first player to cross and mark each sand-trap space with a sticky-note
   — four other team members to cross the grid, avoiding the marked sand traps.
6. If any player steps on a sand trap, the team is immediately disqualified.
7. If all players cross safely, the team receives risk points for finding a safe path, plus "crossing points"—one bonus point for each second *less than* 30 seconds.
8. The team with the most points wins.

Toss Up Game Play

1. Divide the class into two or more teams.
2. Present a five-question quiz on your selected topic.
3. Award each team one toss at the target for each correct response.
4. Scoring:
   — if the Koosh ball lands in the bowl = three points
   — if it lands anywhere else = no points.
5. The team with the most points wins.

This completes our discussion of the four low-tech game formats. Each game has been selected because it's easy to prepare and play. Perhaps the most demanding of the games is Toss Up. So, we've selected this game as our model in the next chapter. This game has been the overwhelming favorite of every business management class at the University of Maryland, Baltimore County, and we want to guide you through its complexities so you can make the best use of it.

Preparing and Playing Your Game

The biggest contributing factor to a game's success is what the trainer does to prepare the game for classroom play.

—Dr. Karen Lawson, *The Trainer's Handbook*

n chapter 3 we identified and then created content (question items) for the learning game experience. In chapter 4 we reviewed the four game formats—manual, card, board, and prop. Now we focus on locating and preparing the materials and props that define the learning game experience, setting up the room, and playing the game.

As a working example throughout this chapter we've selected the prop game Toss Up because this game is (1) a perennial topic-review favorite and (2) an excellent way to illustrate how to set up and play a classroom game. (Additional instructions can be found in chapter 8.) Toss Up demonstrates how preparations, even those that may seem a bit more complicated, can be programmed into just another routine set of steps. And once you've located and prepared the props, preparations for Toss Up are no more difficult than for any other training game.

Game Materials/Props

Materials

Game materials include game boards, question/problem sets, answer sheets, players' instructions, and trainer's master sheets. They can be prepared as wallcharts or

```
┌──────────────────────────────────────┐
│  Game Plan: Working Checklist         │
│                                       │
│    Title: _____   │
│                                       │
│    Format: _____   │
│                                       │
│    Overview:                          │
│      Purpose: _____   │
│      Use: _____   │
│      Audience: _____   │
│      Number of Players: _____   │
│      Time Needed to Play Game: _____  │
│                                       │
│    Game Materials/Props: _____   │
│                                       │
└──────────────────────────────────────┘
```

flipcharts, overhead transparencies, PowerPoint slides, cards, or simply be printed on plain or colored paper.

Game Sheets

For Toss Up, which is played in two or more rounds, all teams receive a game sheet at the start of each round. The game sheet has five content questions, and the teams record their answers to those questions on the game sheets. Remember that in chapter 3 we developed 15 content questions for our classroom game. Because each round of Toss Up uses five questions, we have enough questions for three rounds of play.

To prepare the game sheets for Toss Up, you'll use the sample question sheet shown in the Toss Up instructions in chapter 8. Here are a couple of tips for creating these materials:

- Using a different color of paper to make the game sheets for each round not only adds visual appeal but also helps both the trainer and players keep track of each round of play.
- Make game sheet packets by batching the three game sheets together and distribute one batch to each team before the game starts. This simplifies distribution of materials and speeds up play.

Players' Instructions

Players find it helpful to see the rules of play before and during play. Keeping in mind the eight-sentence-or-fewer rule for instructing your players, simply prepare an overhead transparency, PowerPoint slide, or flipchart page of instructions. For Toss Up, you'll find the players' instructions in chapter 8 and on the accompanying CD.

Trainer's Master Sheet

The master sheet lists the questions—that usually are read aloud during game play—along with the correct responses, rationale behind those responses, and other instructor notes. This is *your* reference sheet, prepare it in whatever way you will find most useful. Here are some ways that master sheets make your game facilitating more successful:

- The first time you use a game or address a new topic, the master sheet helps you organize your thoughts; tracks your time sequences; and reminds you of correct responses, elaborations, and supporting stories.

- The master sheet helps you track game play and keep notes on the quality of the questions (that is, which questions were confusing or out-of-date), on notable participant responses, and on key learning points that you want to emphasize during your question review.

- The master sheet is an instant reference and a starting point for the next time you present this game or topic.

For Toss Up, prepare the master sheets using the same colors of game sheet paper you chose for each round of play.

Props

Although they're tangible and (generally) visible just like game materials, props differ from materials because they're more closely aligned with the "action" component of the game. And there usually is some leeway in selecting props—you can toss a beanbag, a Koosh ball, or some other lightweight object; you can mark your position on a game board with a bottlecap or a button or a wrapped piece of candy. Props offer lots of room for creativity, and they don't have to be pricey. No matter how fancy or how plain they are, props bring a special quality of play to a game.

Some props are not specific to any game, but they create a comfortable and positive climate in the training room. Posters that encourage and energize trainees are props that may not be game specific, but that you may find useful in creating a learning-centered and game-supportive environment. Use message-driven or humorous posters—or some of both. On the team tables, place pitchers of water with glasses, and bowls of wrapped candies (including some that are sugar-free). Paper and pens for note-taking are also useful.

Toss Up is a target qualify-and-score prop game that requires each team to (1) answer the five-question quiz in each round and (2) take the number of target tosses earned by its answers. Players are particularly energized during the hit-or-miss dynamics of the target toss, especially in the final round of play. Here are the props needed for Toss Up:

- standard round soup bowl, measuring from 4 to 6 inches wide, and 2 to 3 inches deep

- Five Koosh balls or beanbags; using softer objects gains higher scores during the target toss because harder objects (tennis or rubber balls, even crumpled paper) tend to bounce out of the target

Trainer's Tip:

You can buy Koosh balls from most toy stores. A very suitable "soft" alternative is the 5-inch urchin ball, which you can find at Trainer's Warehouse (www .trainerswarehouse.com).

◆ double-sided tape to attach the target bowl to the table

◆ masking or painter's tape to create a "throw line" on the floor.

One point we need to make about game props will remind you of our earlier discussion of not calling a game a game: The quality of the props you use *does* matter as you "train up the chain." If you're presenting a learning experience to a group of senior-level executives, your props need more style. Consider replacing your plastic soup bowl or bottle caps with more sophisticated or clever props—how about an ice bucket or wine cooler as a target and golf tees as markers?

Game Equipment

Game Plan: Working Checklist

Title: _____

Format: _____

Overview:
  Purpose: _____
  Use: _____
  Audience: _____
  Number of Players: _____
  Time Needed to Play Game: _____

Game Materials/Props: _____

Equipment: _____

Equipment for a game falls into a category we might think of as "durable goods" (although flipchart paper and marking pens are equipment, too). Equipment comprises larger items that you'll find available in your training space or that you can rent or in some other way arrange to receive and use for training sessions. Here are some examples:

◆ conference and team tables, and chairs

◆ projection equipment

◆ audio and video equipment

◆ flipchart easel(s) with paper and felt-tipped markers.

Be especially careful to arrange for all the projection and audio/visual machinery you'll need for your games. If you're using PowerPoint slides, you'll need a computer to play the presentation and a means for projecting the slides as a large display monitor. You can project overhead transparencies onto a pull-down or free-standing screen, but a light-colored bare wall will work if nothing else is handy. If your game includes an audio- or videotaped component, be sure to cue up and test it before the room is filled with players. Becoming familiar with how all equipment works is vital! And be sure you have a low-tech alternative just in case something crashes and burns.

Let's see what equipment you need for Toss Up. Any standard conference table will serve as the target area where the bowl is placed. The table surface should be 28 to 30 inches off the floor, and it can be round or rectangular. If you're putting your players' instructions and answers/solutions on transparencies or PowerPoint slides, you'll need the appropriate projection equipment. Use an overhead transparency or PowerPoint projector to post the "Players' Instructions" and to present correct answers and solutions. And if you have a felt marker, you can use transparencies to record player comments and observations. If you want to keep the players' instructions visible while you use your electronics to project questions/answers or comments, write the instructions on flipchart paper and mount the flipchart on an easel. Flipcharts also work for recording comments and observations.

Room Setup

Game Plan: Working Checklist

Title: _____

Format: _____

Overview:
   Purpose: _____
   Use: _____
   Audience: _____
   Number of Players: _____
   Time Needed to Play Game: _____

Game Materials/Props: _____

Equipment: _____

Room Setup: _____

When placing a game into the training schedule, it's often a good idea to consider room setup—how much rearranging of the room will a game require, and how much time will it take to break down the game setup and return the room to lecture space? Thoughtful scheduling of breaks can help you avoid a lot of chaos and scrambling.

Getting your training room ready for playing a game is first a matter of considering what you'll be doing before play and what you'll need to use during the game, and then either putting all the elements in place before the training session starts or putting all the elements in a location from which you'll find it convenient to move them into position just before you start the game.

Arrange participant tables and chairs to help the flow of the game. Create as much space as possible between the teams by clustering chairs around tables. This encourages team sharing during the question-and-answer portion of the game.

The pre-game setup for Toss Up should take about 15 minutes. Arrange a play area that's 6 to 8 feet long to accommodate the target table and throwing area. Use a 3-foot strip of painter's tape or quick-release masking tape to define the throwing line. Stick the tape to the floor, parallel to and about 4 feet from the edge of the target table (that's about 1.5 average strides). Place the bowl 12 inches from the table edge closest to the throwing line—this distance from the edge helps keep the tosses on the table and even allows an occasional throw to bounce into the bowl. Because the tossed object can jar or move the bowl, attach the bowl to the table with double-sided tape. (Be sure to have additional tape for emergency re-attachment.) Here's an illustration of the setup for the target toss component of this game:

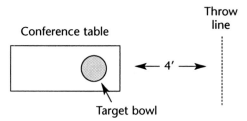

Before Game Play

Game Plan: Working Checklist

Title: _____

Format: _____

Overview:
  Purpose: _____
  Use: _____
  Audience: _____
  Number of Players: _____
  Time Needed to Play Game: _____

Game Materials/Props: _____

Equipment: _____

Room Setup: _____

Before Game Play: _____

The pre-game activities—introductions and team formation—set the mood for game play. A show of interest and enthusiasm should persuade even the most passive participant to enter your nonthreatening learning environment and become an active player. You don't have to be a natural master of ceremonies to rev up spirit; just display genuine interest in the proceedings.

Here's the pre-game action for Toss Up:

* Your first words should welcome your learners to this segment of the lesson plan, informing them that you have a special activity called "Toss Up" you want them to enjoy.
* Divide your participants into two or more teams of at least three players.
* Seat each team at a table or in a conversation area.
* Ask teams to select a team name. (This is optional but many players have told us it was the selection of a team name that was the real invitation to game play.)
* Finally, go over the following players' instructions that you display on an overhead transparency, a slide, or a flipchart:
  — This activity is played in three rounds.
  — In each round, teams have three minutes to respond to five questions on the topic by writing their answers on the game sheet for that round.
  — In each round, time will be called at three minutes and game sheets will be collected.
  — Trainer will present the correct answers and tally team scores after each round, awarding one toss of the Koosh ball for every correct response.
  — Each team selects one member to make its target throw(s).
  — The thrower stands behind the throw line and takes the earned tosses; each toss into the bowl scores three points.
  — Scores are tallied for each round, and the team scoring the most points after three rounds of play wins.

During the Game

Game Plan: Working Checklist

Title: _____

Format: _____

Overview:
 Purpose: _____
 Use: _____
 Audience: _____
 Number of Players: _____
 Time Needed to Play Game: _____

Game Materials/Props: _____

Equipment: _____

Room Setup: _____

Before Game Play: _____

How to Play the Game: _____

Game play is "fun with a purpose." It should contribute to a cohesive and memorable learning experience. It's during game play that your learners become players.

In this section of your Game Plan: Working Checklist, record the order of activities that take place between the start of play and the final call of time or the last team or individual act.

In Toss Up, the first part of the game contains questions on your topic. But it's not an ordinary quiz; rather, it begins as a group race against a three-minute clock. Then, after throws are awarded for correct responses, it becomes an energizing kinesthetic activity—throwing the Koosh ball into the target and scoring points. When scores are posted for the first round, teams are eager to tackle the second (and third) question sets to earn and score in the ensuing rounds. The excitement continues through the third round, where many contests have been won on the very last throw.

To begin game play, you distribute one set of game sheets to each team and ask the teams to write their team name or assigned number on each sheet as an identifier.

Round 1's question-and-answer portion should take six to 10 minutes:

- three minutes to respond to the questions on the game sheet
- one minute to call time and collect the game sheets
- two to six minutes to review the answers and tally the teams' scores.

The second part of round 1 should take 10 to 12 minutes:

- one to two minutes to announce the number of throws each team has earned and to have each team select its thrower
- eight to nine minutes for each thrower to step behind the throw line and take their earned tosses
- one minute for you to tally and post the scores for the round.

The first round ends when the last team's thrower completes her or his tosses. You may want to offer teams three minutes to do some strategic planning for the next two rounds. The second and third rounds repeat the process of round 1.

After three rounds of play, tally all points earned by each team. Announce and congratulate the winning group.

◆   ▪

A game's end opens the way for the next (and some believe most important) stage—debriefing. We think that stage warrants a chapter of its own, and we'll cover the topic in chapter 7. Before we get there, however, let's take time to consider the facilitating role of the instructor. See you in chapter 6.

Trainer's Tip:

During target throws, some players lean toward the target; other players have been known to "inch over" the throw line. To remedy this, simply remind all throwers that stepping over the line disqualifies the throw. Many teams select taller teammates because they think the advantage lies with the lean. This behavior, cited by some as "cheating" and by others as "just playing to win" opens an excellent post-game debriefing dialogue on the topic of fair play.

Role of the Game Facilitator

Learning without thought is labor lost.

—Confucius

During the play of a game, the game facilitator has two roles— managing the game logistics (the task) and managing the group dynamics and the learning (the process). A good facilitator knows how to balance both the task and the process.

- The **task role** in game facilitation involves keeping the game on track, timing the play, tallying the scores, and bringing the game to a close.
- The **process role** in game facilitation requires creating a positive learning climate, setting a tone that ensures participants are comfortable, and managing the level of participation and the group dynamics.

A good facilitator listens well, asks good questions, obtains various viewpoints, and knows when to highlight a learning point.

The facilitator effectively guides the group before, during, and after game play. Tool 6-1 describes some of the work that a facilitator does before, during, and after a game.

The Experiential Learning Cycle

As a facilitator, one of your jobs is to help participants maximize the learning experience from a game. Games are learner-centered rather than teacher-centered activities. What

Tool 6-1: Facilitator Responsibilities Chart

Before the Game	During the Game	After the Game
Introduce the purpose or objective of the game.	Observe behaviors during the game.	Close down game play by tallying points, announcing winners, awarding prizes (optional), and bringing players back to the learning arena.
Explain logistics (the game purpose, rules of play, timing, success factors); distribute game materials; and post rules of play on slides, overhead transparencies, or flipcharts if desired.	Conduct game play, starting and stopping rounds of play; award points; present instruction on the content; present correct responses; assign awards/penalties; resolve questions on game play or content material. When the group gets stuck on a question or problem, resist the urge to solve it for them; allow them some time to figure it out.	
Provide the big picture of how the game relates to your content.	Pay attention to group dynamics— who's participating more than others, how the groups are managing themselves.	Pose the debriefing questions you prepared before the training session. In debriefing the game, focus on what happened, on what was learned, and on what skills and knowledge acquired in the game can be transferred to the real world.
Describe the benefits of playing the game.	Keep the game on track; pay attention to timing and outcome.	Ensure everyone participates in the debriefing.
Provide examples of how the game might be similar to another game to help participants go from "the known" to the "unknown."	Stop the game if the process is breaking down, or if the participants keep trying a solution that doesn't work (in such a case, ask the group "What's happening?" "What might be another way to try this?"); remember not to solve it for them unless there is an unbreakable impasse.	Encourage the sharing of opinions and ideas, and support their diversity.
Seek feedback to ensure that all instructions are understood.	Look for teachable moments that can be discussed after the game.	Focus some of the debriefing time on teachable moments gleaned both from the game content and from player behaviors.
Form teams; explain team roles and provide team instruction sheets (as required).	Keep a neutral presence; don't participate in any of the group discussions or offer your opinion during game play.	Ask for and provide your own examples of how behaviors encountered in the game might apply to real-world experiences.

separates a learner-centered experience from a teacher-centered one is the amount of participant involvement and action. In truly learner-centered training, participants are doing 10 times as much work as the instructor is doing.

The concept of an "Experiential Learning Cycle" was developed by David A. Kolb. Take a look at Figure 6-1.

When we use games in training, it's helpful to consider incorporating the experiential learning cycle throughout. This approach is considered a holistic and integrative approach to learning because it incorporates four different learning stages. Typically, participants will have

1. an immediate or concrete experience that provides the basis for
2. observations and reflections;
3. these observations and reflections are assimilated into theories and concepts, and then
4. applied to real-life work situations.

Stage 1: The Concrete Experience—Learning by Experiencing

After the trainer introduces a learning game and participants are engaged in playing it, the participants are in the "concrete experience" phase of the experiential learning

Figure 6-1. The four stages of Kolb's Experiential Learning Cycle.

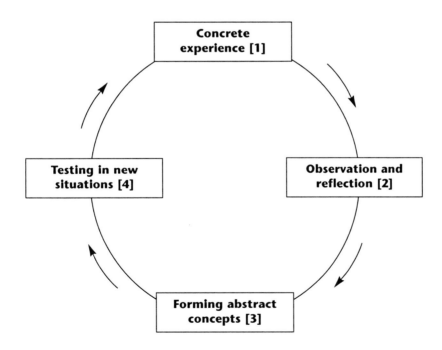

Source: David A. Kolb, *Experiential Learning: Experience as the Source of Learning and Development* (Englewood Cliffs, NJ: Prentice Hall, 1984). Adapted with permission.

cycle. The game creates an opportunity for players to experience the content and theory of the subject matter, either as an introduction to the content or as a review of content previously presented. A game could be used to help new team members learn effective team behaviors. A game could incorporate a task on which all team members need to work together to produce an outcome.

Stage 2: Reflective Observation—Learning by Reflecting

In the "reflective observation" stage of the experiential learning cycle, learners observe their own behaviors and those of others during game play. They view and consider these behaviors from a variety of perspectives. If one of the purposes of a game is to teach roles of effective team members, then players could observe and reflect on how certain individual behaviors helped the team accomplish its goal.

Stage 3: Abstract Conceptualization—Learning by Thinking

Participants process their observations from the game experience and incorporate the concepts and theories presented. If players have observed and reflected on different team behaviors during the game, then they might start making connections to concepts and theories of team role behaviors.

Stage 4: Active Experimentation—Learning by Living It

Participants apply what they have learned in the game experience to the real world. Using the team game experience, players would identify how they might apply what they've learned about effective team behaviors from the game to the ways they could work together more effectively on an upcoming project. They might even assign the roles of the project to individuals who demonstrated those strengths during the game.

Applying the Experiential Learning Cycle to Games

As Thiagi has written, "Anything that can be learned, can be learned from a game." Today's adult learner learns best when she or he is actively engaged with the topic. Learners want to be engaged—they want to try things on their own; to be involved with the key points and concepts; and then, in their own ways, to connect their own dots to internalize the content.

Training games support these desires because they're experiential—they bring the learner into direct contact with the topic in an environment that involves him or her with the content during a real-time learning experience that includes the rules, roles, and behaviors of game play. Games give both the trainer and the learner immediate feedback on the quality of learner input and real-time behavior.

One way to visualize how learning games bring the experiential learning environment to the classroom and create a learner-centered experience is to apply Kolb's Experiential Learning Cycle.

Experiential activities such as games can be the entire method of reaching a training objective or part of several methods. Let's look more closely at how the stages of the learning cycle relate to games (see Tool 6-2).

Learning Styles

Learning styles develop in two ways:

1. how we take in new information or experience
2. how we process what we perceive.

Again looking at Kolb's cycle, learners take in information or experience through (1) **concrete experience**—using intuition or feeling (the "gut") to perceive information; or (2) **abstract conceptualization**—thinking through and analyzing information, taking it in at a cognitive level.

Learners process what they have taken in either through (1) **reflective observation**—observing or reflecting on the experience; or (2) **active experimentation**—jumping in and doing it.

As there are two different ways to take in information and two ways to process information, there are four possible learning styles. Take a look at Figure 6-2.

Tool 6-2: Applying the Experiential Learning Cycle to Games

Stage	Before the Game	During the Game	After the Game
Concrete experience	Prior to game play, the trainer asks participants to pay attention to what they experience during game play.	Participants are actively engaged in the game.	Trainer debriefs participants on what they have experienced and what they have learned around "the experience."
Reflective observation	Trainer tells participants to observe what happens during game play.	Participants observe themselves and others—behaviors, reactions, and learning.	Trainer prompts reflection by asking participants to write down what they have observed and then discuss their observations as a large group.
Abstract conceptualization	Trainer asks participants to pay attention to concepts or theories that relate to the topic of the game.	The content of the game reinforces theories or concepts presented prior or after the game.	Trainer asks participants to relate what they have learned during game play to the key concepts of the topic.
Active experimentation	The trainer describes how and why the game relates to actual life experience.	Participants begin to identify how they might apply what they're learning in the game experience.	Trainer asks participants to describe how they will apply what they have learned in the game to real-life situations.

Figure 6-2. Learning styles within the context of Kolb's Experiential Learning Cycle.

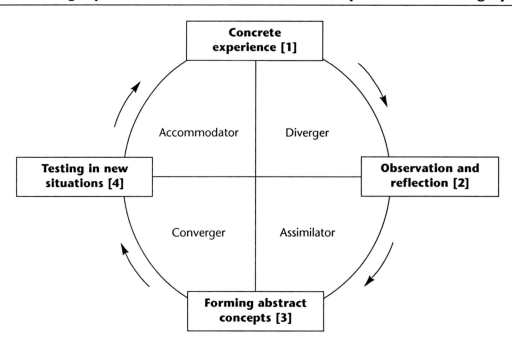

Source: David A. Kolb, *Experiential Learning: Experience as the Source of Learning and Development* (Englewood Cliffs, NJ: Prentice Hall, 1984). Adapted with permission.

A **diverger** combines the learning steps of concrete experience and reflective observation. A **converger** combines active experimentation and abstract conceptualization. An **assimilator** combines the learning steps of abstract conceptualization and reflective observation. And an **accommodator** combines concrete experience and active experimentation.

Your participants will have personal preferences for how they learn, and it's interesting to consider how different learning styles will show up during game play. Look at Tool 6-3 for typical behaviors associated with the various learning styles.

Every trainer also has her or his own learning style, and bias toward that preference can creep into the way a game is facilitated. It's important that you avoid such bias and maintain a balance among the learning approaches so that you provide opportunities for all your players to take in and process the information you offer and to participate and learn from the games they play in your training sessions.

For more information on learning styles using the Experiential Learning Cycle, visit David A. Kolb's Website: http://www.learningfromexperience.com. This Website includes the latest research on experiential learning and how to obtain the Kolb Learning Style Inventory.

Tool 6-3: Typical Behaviors Associated with Learning Styles

The Accommodator	The Diverger
• Has the ability to learn from hands-on experience • Loves to take risks • Enjoys looking at things from many perspectives • Tends to be adaptable and practical • May act on gut feelings	• Has the ability to view concrete situations from many different points of view • Tends to observe rather than take action • Enjoys activities that call for generating ideas • Often prefers working in groups • Is sensitive to feelings
The Converger	**The Assimilator**
• Is best at finding practical uses for ideas and theories • Has the ability to solve problems and make decisions based on finding solutions • Likes to deal with technical tasks rather than social or interpersonal issues	• Is best at understanding a wide range of information and putting it into a concise logical form • Often is interested in abstract ideas and concepts • Develops theories • Defines problems

Debriefing the Games

Everyone can use a game provided that there is a relevant learning point.

—Colleen Carruthers, The TR Group

Game Plan: Working Checklist

Title: _____

Format: _____

Overview:
  Purpose: _____
  Use: _____
  Audience: _____
  Number of Players: _____
  Time Needed to Play Game: _____

Game Materials/Props: _____

Equipment: _____

Room Setup: _____

Before Game Play: _____

How to Play the Game: _____

After Game Play—Debriefing:

Why Debrief a Game?

Debriefing a game can be the richest part of the entire process. Whether the game has gone well or gone poorly, learning has occurred. You can enhance and maximize that learning with proper debriefing. If you're tempted to skip the debriefing because the game has invoked high energy or because players seemed fully engaged with the game, don't do it. Every game experience is sharpened by asking

- "What happened?"
- "What did you experience?"
- "What did you learn?"
- "What would you change the next time around?"

The debriefing can be considered the most important part of the game process because it integrates the learning of the content, observations of behaviors, and application to real-world situations.

Questions: The Debriefing Key

The key tool that a facilitator uses to debrief is questions. They allow for reflection, giving an opportunity for the learner to step back and process what he or she has taken in. Questions also prompt engagement and participation from the players. By asking questions, both the facilitator and the learner can identify what's been learned.

The two different types of questions that are asked in debriefing are open ended and closed ended. An **open-ended** question has many possible answers. A **closed-ended** question often has a specific answer, such as a yes or no, true or false.

Open-ended questions are preferred during a debriefing to maximize participation and enhance learning. These types of questions are more helpful in drawing out participation from everyone. The facilitator generally is asking broadly about the learning experience encountered in the game, and there can be many answers. The facilitator wants to elicit from the players as much as possible about their experience with the game and the learning that has taken place.

- Open-ended questions begin with "who," "what," "how," "when," and "where." Use them when you want to increase individual or group participation and involvement in the debriefing or to intensify the level of discussion. It often is helpful to ask an open-ended question to probe deeper into a response. Frequently these questions are directed to the whole group to maximize participation.
- Closed-ended questions often can be answered with a single word, so when you want to limit participation or end discussion, use a closed-ended question.

Here are the three key uses of debriefing questions:

1. to keep participants involved
2. to create an opportunity for everyone to express ideas and opinions
3. to give the trainer and the participants feedback on what content has been retained.

Applying the Experiential Learning Cycle to the Debriefing

To get the greatest benefit from the debriefing experience, the facilitator can follow the four stages of Kolb's Experiential Learning Cycle (covered in chapter 6) in processing the game. To do this, ask questions that pertain to each part of the cycle. Here are some examples:

Stage 1: Process the experience (concrete experience)

Sample debriefing questions:

- What happened?
- What did you experience?
- What did you feel?

Stage 2: Provide an opportunity for reflection (reflective observation)

Sample debriefing question:

- Take a moment and think about what happened here. What did you observe?
- What else did you notice?

Stage 3: Integrate concepts into theories (abstract conceptualization)

Sample debriefing questions:

- How does this game relate to the theory that we discussed earlier?
- How did the game draw out some of the concepts that we have been discussing?

Stage 4: Integrate the game experience into real-world application (active experimentation)

Sample debriefing question:

- How would this game experience apply to situations that you face at work?

Tips for Success in the Debriefing Process

- **Plan ahead.** Choose questions for use in the debriefing ahead of time to ensure that you get the results you're looking for. Think about the answer you're seeking, and then design your question to elicit that answer. Your goal is to guide the participant to the correct answer. A question that's too broad or too narrow will make it difficult for the player to answer.

    You also may tailor questions that are more specific to the learning outcome. Tailor your questions to the group's overall experience level. You want to encourage participation, not make the questions too easy or too difficult for the group to answer. An entry-level salesperson may be asked,

Trainer's Tip:

Make notes when you are observing the game. This will help you tailor your questions to the participants' experience.

"What helped you solve the problem here?" whereas a more experienced salesperson may be asked, "How does the problem-solving experience in this game relate to your client situations?"

As you plan your debriefing, keep in mind what learning points you would like the group to discuss. Choose questions from the sample debrief questions provided in Tool 7-1, and add in other questions of your own that will maximize the learning process. You want to make sure that everyone has a chance to process the personal experience of the game.

◆ **Bring the group together into one large class before you start the debriefing.** This may be done as easily as saying in an upbeat manner, "Let's get back together now!" When the game has created a lot of energy in the room, however, it can be difficult to bring the group back for discussion. If this is the case, you may want to try these options:

— Give participants a five-minute break. This will bring their energy back into normal range when they settle back into their seats.

Tool 7-1: Sample Debriefing Questions for Each Stage of the Experiential Learning Cycle

Initial questions:
- How was it?
- What did you enjoy most?

Stage 1: Concrete Experience
- What happened?
- How do you feel?
- How did you feel when . . . ?
- What did you experience?
- Who else feels the same way about that? How come?
- When did you feel challenged?

Stage 2: Reflective Observation
- What did you observe about the game?
- What did you observe about yourself?
- What did you see others doing?
- What did you notice about . . . ?
- What other solutions did you consider?
- When did you really see that you were working as a team?
- When did you observe challenges?

Stage 3: Abstract Conceptualization
- How does this game relate to some of the concepts presented so far?
- How does all this fit together?
- What new insights do you have?
- What parts of this game seemed similar to what you already know about the topic?

Stage 4: Active Experimentation
- How can you apply what you've learned from this game to your work situation?
- What will you do differently as a result of playing this game?
- If you were to play this game again, what would you do differently?
- What did you learn about yourself? About the group?
- What might you need to watch out for as you apply these techniques in the future?
- What will really help you apply some of the strategies that you learned in this game?
- When might you apply what you've learned from this game?

— Use chimes, a bell, or some other type of noisemaker to draw the group's attention.

— Say, "If you can hear me, start clapping." Do this until the entire room is clapping and attention is focused back on you.

◆ **Allow a moment for reflection.** When all of the participants have been brought back together, take a moment for everyone to collect their thoughts. You might say, "Take a little time to think about this activity. Think about what happened, what you observed, what you learned, and so forth." You might even ask participants to jot down a few notes. Allowing for brief reflection time before beginning the debriefing discussion helps ensure that everyone participates, and helps those players who might need a bit of time to process their thoughts before speaking. A richer discussion often results from more reflection time.

◆ **Sequence your questions.** Ask questions in a pattern of increasing difficulty or complexity. Easier questions at the beginning will help engage the entire group and give more opportunities for everyone to participate.

◆ **Revisit the purpose or objective of your game.** Some games are designed for the learning objective and purpose to be discovered during the game. Such a discovery approach to learning often enables players to achieve some predetermined conclusion and leads to the well-known "aha!" If your game takes this approach, ask players if they have discovered the envisioned key outcome of the game. If the game's purpose was not to be discovered during game play, then discuss the purpose with the group, and ensure that everyone has understood the connection between the game and the content of the workshop.

◆ **Ensure that everyone participates:**
— Manage equal group participation by paying attention to who is speaking and who you might need to draw out.

— Place yourself at the center of the room and try to get as close to your participants as you can. A rule of thumb is to be able to see the entire group within your peripheral vision. Getting close to your participants will encourage their engagement.

— If a player from one side of the room is answering a question, walk to the opposite side of the room while maintaining eye contact so that the participant will be heard by the entire group.

— It's helpful to ask open-ended questions initially to encourage participation; then follow up with more probing questions. Open-ended questions directed to the entire group encourage participation because there are no right or wrong answers, and everyone is invited to discuss his or her experiences. These questions generally create a safe environment. For example, when you ask, "What did you experience?" each person may have a different answer because he or she may have had a different experience, and that's OK. A facilitator can always follow up that question by asking, "How many of you also experienced this?"

- **When responding to participants, give positive feedback.** Be careful, however, not to make one person's comments seem more important or valuable than others. Maintain your neutrality because your role is to get as much input as possible from the group—not provide your own opinion. Help guide the discussion and ensure that learning has occurred.

- **When asking and answering questions, follow these suggestions:**
  — If you're directing questions to individual class members, it's helpful to use their names first so their attention is drawn to the question and no one gets surprised or embarrassed. For example: "John, how will you apply what you've learned from this game?"
  — If no one answers your question, it may be that the question is unclear. Try reframing the question and ask again.
  — Try not to answer the questions yourself. Participants often need some time to think. If you grow impatient and start answering your own questions, participation will come to a halt!

- **Make the most of teachable moments.** While observing the game in process, you may have seen a teachable moment occurring. Highlighting in the debriefing a particular situation you observed during game play can illuminate a concrete learning example.

- **Keep the group's engagement level high** during the debriefing, and recognize when it's time to finish by gauging the group's attention level.

- **Manage group dynamics appropriately** to keep discussions on track. See Tool 7-2 for helpful suggestions to avoid distracting or monopolizing behaviors.

Other Formats for Debriefing

There are several other formats you can use for debriefing to add variety to the experience. If you want to keep the discussion format, you might add one of these activities to it.

List Building

Purpose: To provoke reflection before debriefing the game

Materials: Paper and pens for notetaking, a chart or whiteboard, and markers

Tool 7-2: Managing Group Dynamics

Situation	Solution
One person dominates the discussion.	Thank the person quickly. Then turn your body slightly toward someone else and ask a question of that player. Use participants' names. Say the name first, then ask the question. For example: "Thanks, John! Sarah, what's your opinion on this?"
The energy of the group seems low.	Tell the group that the energy in the room seems low. Ask what people believe might be causing or contributing to this?
Participation is lacking.	If one or two players seem reluctant to engage, ask them easy yes/no questions, or ask for their opinions. For example: "Ken, do you agree with this?"
There is aggressive, angry behavior, or a difficult participant.	If this happens at any time during the game process, call a break and talk to that person privately. If the person continues to disrupt the group, you may need to ask the person to leave.
Someone provides a wrong answer to a question.	Rephrase and ask the question again. Offer an example and ask again. Redirect the question to the group, and then go back to that individual to see if he or she can give you another answer. Avoid telling players that they're wrong. This may shut down participation, and it could be that the question was unclear or that they misunderstood the original question.

Process:

- Pose a question to the group and tell them you want to build a list of possible answers.
- Ask participants to build their individual list first (to give them some reflection time).
- Walk around and check to see what's appearing on their lists.
- Ask one person to start—ideally someone who has written something you'd like to address.
- Build the list quickly on a chart or a whiteboard.
- As you build the list on the chart or whiteboard, use a dash or a bullet for each point instead of a number. A number can indicate a priority, and one idea is not more important than another.
- When you've exhausted everyone's personal lists, add some points of your own if needed to stimulate further discussion.

Reflective Questions: What?/So What?/Now What?

This approach parallels the experiential learning cycle by following the order of these questions.

Purpose: To promote discussion that reviews the details of the experience, and moves toward critical thinking, problem solving, and applying learning from the game to the real world

Process: You can ask these questions of individuals or of the group as a whole; they work equally well for discussion and for journaling.

What?

+ The questions seeks a descriptive response.
+ Facts: what happened, with whom?
+ What did you experience?
+ How did it feel?

So What?

+ The question shifts from description to interpretation.
+ Meaning of experience for each participant.
+ What feelings were involved, and what lessons were learned?

Now What?

+ The question asks for context; seeks a sense of this situation's place in the big picture.
+ Setting future goals, applying experiences to the future.

Structured Journaling

Purpose: To use reflection in response to journal questions

Materials: A journal and pen

Process: Ask your players to think of a recent event or circumstance, and to answer the following questions about it. Have them write their answers in their journals, taking three to four minutes for each response.

+ What did I do that worked?
+ What did I do that didn't work?
+ What do I feel?
+ What were my assumptions or beliefs at that time?
+ What was motivating me?
+ What else could I have done?
+ What alternative attitudes or behaviors could I adopt?
+ What will I do next time?

Sentence Stems

In addition to prompting a discussion, this activity can be used as a closure activity after the debriefing discussion to wrap up the topic.

Purpose: To help participants reflect on their experience

Materials: Flipchart for writing sentence stems, or prepared worksheets

Process: Ask class members to complete the following sentence stems. Options include writing the answers in their journals, sharing them individually with the whole group, or answering as a group.

- "Today, I learned . . . "
- "I feel . . . "
- "This game gave me . . . "

Closing the Debriefing Discussion

Thank participants for their involvement. Make sure before the debriefing discussion is finished that key learning points have been processed and that the game has been tied back to the original topic. Be certain to call at least a brief break between the end of the debriefing and the start of additional work.

Sample Closure Activities

Ask individuals to describe with one word any of these aspects of the game (be sure you ask each person in the group):

- their experience
- their overall reaction to the game
- what had the most impact
- what new ideas came to light.

Games for Classroom Play

*Come play my classroom game
And see with smiling eyes
The race that is more fun
Than winning or a prize.*

—Steve Sugar, *Primary Games*

We now present for your use and re-use a "starter set" of 11 classroom-tested, classroom-proven training games. Each game brings its own, unique approach to classroom learning in terms of format, use, and play. The playlist includes

- a no-fail icebreaker—Signature Hunt
- team icebreaker/creativity games—Bingo Hunt and Match Point
- a handout review/preview game—Review Bingo
- instant topic reviews—Quiz Challenge and Tic-Tac-Topic
- a team play-and-review game—Toss Up
- a team learning/topic review game—Get-Set
- an individual problem-solving/team-play game—Card Sort
- a team problem-solving/risk-taking game—Sand Trap
- a board game review—Board Bingo.

Tool 8-1 is a matrix that points out the various uses for each of the games. It will help you choose games that suit your purpose.

Tool 8-1: Game Use Matrix

	Content Application	Creativity	Icebreaker	Interteam play	New content introduction	Problem solving	Content review	Vocabulary review	Risk taking	Team learning
Bingo Hunt		X	X	X		X				X
Board Bingo				X	X		X	X	X	
Card Sort	X			X	X	X	X	X		X
Get-Set		X		X		X				X
Match Point		X	X	X	X	X			X	X
Quiz Challenge	X			X	X		X	X	X	
Review Bingo					X		X	X		
Sand Trap			X	X		X			X	X
Signature Hunt			X							
Tic-Tac-Topic	X				X		X	X		
Toss Up	X			X			X	X	X	X

For your convenience, each game follows the guidelines established by the Game Plan: Working Checklist, with specific tips on props, materials, setup, and game play from introduction—including a ready-to-copy set of players' instructions and a set of suggested post-play debriefing questions.

Title: Bingo Hunt

This is an energizing "scavenger hunt" activity using the familiar bingo frame. Each team receives a bingo-style game sheet containing clues or references to specific items. Each team then locates or produces items that satisfy the clues on the game sheet. The team that covers the most game sheet spaces wins.

Format: Manual game

Overview:

Purpose: To challenge the participants intellectually

Uses: Creativity, icebreaker, interteam play, problem solving, team learning

Audience: Any level

Number of Players: 6 or more

Time Needed to Play Game: 15 to 30 minutes

Game Materials/Props:

- *For each team:*
    - 1 game sheet with 25 clues placed in a 5 x 5-space bingo-frame layout
    Suggested Clues: Use descriptions or short phrases that are open to interpretation to encourage problem solving and creativity. (Please see Tool 8-2.)
    - 1 pencil or highlight marker

- *For the instructor:*
    - a master sheet of the clues, a list of suggested item(s) that meet the clue requirements, and other notes as needed
    - an overhead transparency, PowerPoint slide, or flipchart page displaying the Players' Instructions.

Equipment:

- Overhead projector, or computer and projection/display monitor
- Flipchart with easel and felt-tipped markers for tallying scores and posting player comments and observations (optional).

Room Setup: For best results, provide a table and chairs for each team.

Before Game Play:

1. Divide group into two or more teams of three to seven players each.
2. Distribute one game sheet and one pencil or highlight marker to each team.

Trainer's Tip:

Game sheets of 25 clues placed on a 5 x 5-space layout can be prepared using the "Table" toolbar in Windows 2000 and up. Create a five-row by five-column table (auto-fit to window), and fill in each space with your clue about an item that can be located or produced by each team, such as items found in the training room; on their group table; or in wallets, purses, or clothing.

Game Plan: Working Checklist

Title:
Format:
Overview:
  Purpose:
  Use:
  Audience:
  Number of Players:
  Time Needed to Play Game:
Game Materials/Props:
Equipment:
Room Setup:
Before Game Play:
How to Play the Game:
After Game Play—Debriefing:

Tool 8-2: Sample Bingo Hunt Game Sheet

Directions: Find specific items named or things that fit the descriptions provided in each square.

Newsworthy	Sweet	Toy-like	Minty	International
Plastic	Scratchy	Golden	Flowery	Official document
Silvery	Brand or tattoo	Sandy	Etching	Sticky
Metallic	Purple	Logo	Insect product	Seasonal
Circular	Limerick	Stately	Trashy	Tuneful

How to Play the Game:

1. Announce the task:
    a. Each team must provide items that satisfy the clues in the spaces on the game sheet. (*Note to trainer:* Teams may start with any clue they wish. Remind them that it is not the pattern but the number of covered spaces that determines the winner.)
    b. Teams must find in the room or must create each item and must explain how each item satisfies its clue.
2. Teams may choose to work as a unit or separate into subunits to create items for specific clues. This can lead to examples of team problem solving and to self-directed teams.
3. When the team locates an item, it covers the appropriate space by marking an "X" through that space.

4. Give teams 15 minutes to cover as many game sheet spaces as they can.

5. The first team to cover all the spaces on its game sheet wins.

6. If time of play expires with no winners, ask each team how many spaces they have covered and select as the winner the team with the most covered spaces.

Here are some examples from the game sheet found in Tool 8-2:

*   "Newsworthy"—a newspaper article or a current event (such as a team member who has recently become a parent or bought a new home)

*   "Tuneful"— a cell phone tune or the written words "Happy Birthday to You" (sung on request)

*   "Etching"—an etched picture from a book or magazine or the portrait on paper currency.

After Game Play—Debriefing:

Sample debriefing questions:

*   What did you experience?
*   What happened?
*   What helped you come up with the solutions?
*   What did you learn?
*   How will you apply what you learned?

Game Note:

*   Depending on time and/or class members, you may want to consider one of these winning patterns as alternatives to covering the entire sheet:

    — cover five spaces in a row, vertically, horizontally, or corner-to-corner

    — cover all the spaces around the edge (also called a picture frame)

    — cover all the inside spaces (also called a nine-pack).

PLAYERS' INSTRUCTIONS FOR
Bingo Hunt

1. Form teams of three or more players.

2. Each team receives a game sheet and a pencil or marker.

3. Find or create an item that satisfies the clue for that space.

4. When you produce an item that satisfies the space's clue requirement, mark an "X" through the appropriate space.

5. When time is called, the team with the most spaces covered wins.

Title: Board Bingo

This fast-playing board game pits two opposing teams at a bingo-style game board in their quest to be the first team to cover five spaces in a row. Game play involves teams rolling a die, selecting a game board space, and then earning that space by correctly answering your topic question.

Format: Board game

Overview:

Purpose: To reveal the learner's level of understanding of the topic

Uses: Interteam play, new content introduction, content review, vocabulary review, risk taking

Audience: Any level

Number of Players: 8 or more

Time Needed to Play Game: 20 to 35 minutes

Game Materials/Props:

- 25 topic questions (listed two to an overhead transparency, one per PowerPoint slide, or written on flipchart paper)
  Suggested Question Types: Short answer, multiple-choice, (using only two or three choices), and true-false. See question tips in the Game Notes.
- *For each set of two teams:*
  — 1 game board (see Tool 8-3; print the game board from the accompanying CD-ROM. To create a sturdier game board, print onto cover stock [75-pound paper], laminate both sides, or attach to a cardboard or foamcore backing.)
  — 15 red and 15 white chips (available at toy or game stores)
  — 1 red and 1 white die (available at toy or game stores).
- *For the instructor:*
  — a master sheet of the correct responses and other notes as needed
  — an overhead transparency, PowerPoint slide, or flipchart page displaying the Players' Instructions.

Equipment:

- Overhead projector, or computer and projection/display monitor
- Flipchart with easel and felt-tipped markers.

Game Plan: Working Checklist

Title: ....

Format: ....

Overview:
Purpose: ....
Use: ....
Audience: ....
Number of Players: ....
Time Needed to Play Game: ....

Game Materials/Props: ....

Equipment: ....

Room Setup: ....

Before Game Play: ....

How to Play the Game: ....

After Game Play--Debriefing: ....

Trainer's Tip:

Most teams prefer to select their own color of die and chips. If necessary, assign one team as the "red" team, and the other team as the "white" team—both teams now using the as-signed color die and chips.

Tool 8-3: Board Bingo Game Board

1	4	5	3	2
2	5	3	1	4
3	2	4	5	1
4	3	1	2	5
5	1	2	4	3

©The Game Group, 2000

Room Setup: For best results, provide a conference or small game table (with chairs) where two teams can face each other with the game board, chips, and dice between them.

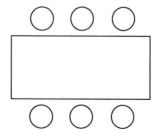

Before Game Play:

- Distribute one set of game materials to each table.
- Divide the group into two teams of two or three players each.
- Have two teams meet at each game board.
- Have each team select one red or white die and matching red or white chips.

How to Play the Game:

1. Have each team select a team captain. The captain is responsible for presenting the "final" team answer to each question. The captain is also responsible for determining who rolls the team die by assigning a designated roller or rotating the roll among team members.

2. Red team rolls its die and selects a space matching the number rolled. (For example, if the team rolls a "4" it may select any open "4" space on the game board by putting its die as a "placeholder" on the selected space until the question-answer process is completed.) Rolling a "6" lets the team select any open space it chooses.

3. The trainer presents the first question by reading the question shown on overhead, PowerPoint slide, or flipchart. Players say that it is helpful to both see *and* hear the question presented.

4. After the question has been read aloud, the red team captain has 30 seconds to give his or her answer to the opposing team.

5. The trainer gives the correct answer.

6. If the red team's answer is *correct,* it removes the die and places a red chip on its selected space. If *incorrect,* the red team removes its die; no chip is placed on the selected space.

7. Play then alternates to the white team, which rolls the white die, selects a space, and answers the next question.

8. Play alternates back-and-forth after every question until one team at each game board covers five spaces in a row, horizontally, vertically, or diagonally.

Trainer's Tip:

Teams should use the die (not a chip) as the "placeholder." This eliminates confusion over which space is being earned and allows the "winner's" ritual of replacing the die with a chip.

After Game Play—Debriefing:

Sample debriefing questions:

- How was it?
- How do you feel?
- What did you experience?
- What helped you answer the questions?
- How did you work together?
- What would you do differently next time?
- How will you apply what you've learned?

Game Notes:

- ◆ In later game play, if one team rolls its die and all the spaces matching that number are covered, have the team roll again. If there is no available space matching the second roll, the team loses its turn.

- ◆ Having teams use different color chips and dice helps the trainer see the status of play without interrupting the game.

- ◆ When devising your questions and answers, include the rationale along with the correct response to take advantage of the "moment of learning" that occurs when the correct answer is presented.

- ◆ Here are some sample questions,* with sales management as the topic:

  — *Question:* The term used to describe the loss due to shoplifting is _____. *Answer:* Shrinkage, or shrink. The terms describe stock that cannot be accounted for in the record-keeping system.

  — *Question:* A customer in a retail store appears to be "browsing." The best sales tactic is (a) not to interrupt or (b) to offer assistance. *Answer:* (b) Offer assistance. Letting a customer know that you're available and standing by can create a conversation that may lead to a sale. It also discourages shoplifting.

  — *Question:* Name the marketing method that sends a brochure or letter to a large number of possible new clients. *Answer:* Direct mail. With this approach, the sales generated need to exceed the cost of printing and postage enough to create a reasonable profit.

---

*Questions courtesy of Dr. Linda Dillon Jones, director of training and education, the Johns Hopkins University, Baltimore.

PLAYERS' INSTRUCTIONS FOR
Board Bingo

1. Divide group into sets of two teams, each with two or three players.

2. Each team chooses a captain and selects a die and matching chips

3. Red team throws its die and selects matching game board space by placing its die on the selected space.

4. Red team responds to the first question.

5. If response is *correct,* remove die and cover space with red chip. If response is *incorrect,* remove die.

6. White team rolls its die and responds to the next question.

7. All rounds are played the same.

8. The first team to cover five spaces in a row wins.

Title: Card Sort

This sorting game, played on a wall chart, is designed to improve recognition of similarities and differences among the topic items. In relay-style race against time, each player must decide and place his or her card into the correct category before the next player can play his or her card. The team with the most correctly placed cards wins.

Format: Card game

Overview:

Purpose: To demonstrate knowledge or understanding of the topic

Uses: Content application, interteam play, new content introduction, problem solving, content review, vocabulary review, team learning

Audience: Any level

Number of Players: 10 or more

Time Needed to Play Game: 15 to 35 minutes

Game Materials/Props:

- *For each team:*
  — 1 game chart placed on the wall or on a flipchart easel (See our example chart and item cards for a sorting game of Odds and Evens in Tool 8-4.)
  — 1 set of 11 to 19 index cards, with one clue on each card. (Each clue should provide enough information to enable a player to place the card in an appropriate category. For instance, if the two categories were "Safe Working Condition" or "Unsafe Working Condition," an unsafe-condition card might read "Open Cans of Paint." Use a different color of cards for each team, if possible.)

- *For the instructor:*
  — a master sheet listing each item, its correct category, and additional notes as needed
  — an overhead transparency, PowerPoint slide, or flipchart sheet displaying the Players' Instructions
  — 1 roll (or several strips) of masking or painter's tape.

Equipment:

- Overhead projector, or computer and projection/display monitor
- Flipchart with easel and felt-tipped markers to tally scores and post player comments and observations (optional).

Room Setup: Using easy-to-remove masking or painter's tape, hang up a game wallchart for each team, leaving enough intervening wall space to avoid crowding. *Alternative:* Set up a flipchart on an easel for each team. Place one wallchart on each easel.

Trainer Tip:

This game is an excellent way to present the similarities/ differences of a variety of "either-or" topics, such as true or false (any topic), safe versus unsafe (plant safety, vehicle operation and repair), appropriate or inappropriate behavior (sexual harassment, product sales, call center work), legal versus illegal (business, accounting practices), and so forth.

Tool 8-4: Sample Card Sort Chart and Item Cards

Odds	Evens

$125 coat on sale
@ 20% discount =

75 x 60% + 2 =

10% of 140 + (2 x 1.50) =

Before Game Play:

1. Divide the group into teams of five to nine players.
2. Have each team meet at one of the wallcharts or easels.
3. Place a set of item cards face down on a chair or table beside each wallchart or easel.
4. Provide a roll or strips of masking tape to each team to be used to attach the item cards to the wallchart.
5. Have each team's members line up in single file at its wallchart or easel.

How to Play the Game:

1. Announce the task: "This exercise is a review of the basic mental math skills you need for sales management. Each card contains a calculation that totals to either an "odd" or "even" number. Each player must pick up the top card, make his or her calculation, and place the card in either the odd or even category *before* the next player can touch a card. Each team has two minutes to correctly sort as many cards as it can."

2. On your signal, the first player in each team's line turns over the top card, calculates the math problem, and attaches it in the appropriate place on the chart.

3. When the first card is placed, the second player takes and places the next card.

4. Play continues in the same way for the rest of the players until you call time at two minutes.

5. As you go over the correct answers, have each team remove all incorrectly placed cards from the wallchart.

6. Have each team tally the remaining (correctly placed) cards.

7. Award one point for each correctly placed card.

8. The team with the most points wins.

After Game Play—Debriefing:

Sample debriefing questions:

- How was this activity?
- What did you enjoy the most?
- What happened?
- What helped your progress?
- What hindered your progress?
- What did you learn about teamwork?
- How does this game relate to what we discussed earlier?
- How will you use in the future what you've learned here?

Game Notes:

- Use alternate scoring, if needed:
  - correct placement = + one point
  - incorrect placement = – one point.
- Play more than one round (using different card sets). Allow teams to strategize between rounds.

PLAYERS' INSTRUCTIONS FOR
Card Sort

1. Divide into two or more teams.

2. When instructed, the first player turns over the first card.

3. The first player places the card in the appropriate column on the wallchart.

4. When the first player has completed this task, the second player turns over the next card.

5. Play continues until time is called at two minutes.

6. Teams receive one point for each correctly placed card.

7. The team with the most points wins.

Title: Get-Set

This is an absorbing team learning game in which each team must solve an entire set of five topic problems or face a penalty. The punitive scoring system and the round-by-round interteam competition create an interesting dialogue on team productivity and team behavior.

Format: Manual game

Overview:

Purpose: To demonstrate problem-solving skills in a team setting

Uses: Creativity, interteam play, problem solving, team learning

Audience: Any level, but especially suited to new or existing work teams

Number of Players: 10 or more

Time Needed to Play Game: 25 to 90 minutes

Game Materials/Props:

- ◆ *For each team:*
  - — Pencils and scratch paper
  - — 1 game sheet per team member for each round of play (This enables each team to work as a group or as individuals to solving the problem set.)
    To prepare the game sheets: Devise one set of five problems for each round of play. Problem sets may include questions on the training topic, on new product information (sales), on plant or workplace information/jargon, math calculations, and so forth. (See Tool 8-5 for an example—one round of questions on customer relations.) If possible, use different colors of paper for each round (for easier handling and play). Collate each team's game sheets for each round. If you have three teams, you should have three packets of game sheets for each round of play.

- ◆ *For the instructor:*
  - — a master sheet of each round's game sheet, including the correct responses, the rationale for each response, and any useful instructor's notes
  - — an overhead transparency, PowerPoint slide, or flipchart page displaying the Players' Instructions
  - — a two-minute timer, stopwatch, or watch with a second hand
  - — an overhead transparency, PowerPoint slide, or flipchart page displaying the correct responses (optional)
  - — noisemaker, whistle, or chimes (optional).

Tool 8-5: Sample Get-Set Game Sheet

Team _____ Round No. _____

Topic: Customer Relations

1. Many jobs in the service sector require _____ skills even more than technical skills.
2. Customer-contact employees need feedback more often than do employees on the production line. True or false?
3. What happens to service "extras" as they are adopted by others in the same industry?
4. The most important skill to use in providing good customer service is:
   a. smiling
   b. listening
   c. product knowledge
5. When customers evaluate coffee service at a conference held in a hotel, what do they find to be most important?

Answers:

1. Social or interpersonal
2. True. They often need feedback weekly, even daily.
3. They become the service norm in the industry.
4. Listening
5. Near phones, near restrooms, quick service

Equipment:

- Overhead projector, or computer and projection/display monitor
- Flipchart with easel and felt-tipped markers to tally scores and post player comments and observations (optional).

Room Setup: For best results, provide a table and chairs for each team.

Before Game Play:

1. Divide group into teams of five to six players.
2. Seat each team at its own table.

How to Play the Game:

1. Distribute pencils and the first round of five problems to each team.
2. Tell teams they have two minutes to solve the five problems. Start the clock.
3. Call time at the end of two minutes.
4. Review the correct solutions.
5. (a) Award five points to each team that solves *all five* problems; (b) penalize by three points each team that *does not solve all five* problems.

6. Distribute problems for the next round and continue play in the same manner for all rounds, scoring after each round.
7. When all rounds are completed, tally team points. The team with the most points wins.

After Game Play—Debriefing:

Sample debriefing questions:

- What happened?
- How did your team work together?
- How did you apply some of the problem-solving concepts?
- What else did you learn about problem solving here?
- How might you apply some of those problem-solving skills? In what situations?

Game Notes:

- The scoring system's "negative" construct reflects an "all-or-nothing" business attitude. This could be an interesting post-game discussion.
- We use five-question sets because many teams roll through four of the questions, but seem to struggle with one of the five questions. This struggle helps with team learning issues.
- Here are some suggested problem sets:
  — vocabulary questions
  — topic questions—short answer questions only, not multiple-choice or true-false.
- Schedule planning meetings between rounds so that teams can evaluate and, if necessary, alter the way they're working. You could help them by having the team ask themselves this: "To achieve better results in the next round, what should we [start doing?] [stop doing?] [continue doing?]"

PLAYERS' INSTRUCTIONS FOR
Get Set

1. Divide into teams of five or six players.

2. In each round, you have two minutes to solve a set of five problems.

3. If you correctly solve all five problems, you receive five points.

4. If you correctly solve four or fewer problems, you are penalized three points.

5. All rounds are played the same way.

6. The team with the most points at the end of the final round wins.

Title: Match Point

This is an excellent warm-up exercise that requires teams to brainstorm "theme" items suggested by the match of a letter to a category. Use this game once, or in rounds, to preview team problem solving and creativity.

Format: Prop game

Overview:

Purpose: To challenge the participants intellectually

Uses: Creativity, icebreaker, interteam play, new content introduction, problem solving, risk taking, team learning

Audience: Any level

Number of Players: 8 or more

Time Needed to Play Game: 20 to 40 minutes

Game Materials/Props:

* *For each team:*
  — one wallchart made from flipchart paper
    To make the wallchart: Write the overall theme at the top of the chart. Use any theme that opens a dialogue about an important topic or concept, such as product information or plant safety. Pick two to five categories fitting the theme, and write them down the left side of the chart; draw horizontal lines to separate the categories. Select three or four alphabet letters, and create vertical columns with one letter at the top of each column; draw vertical lines to separate the columns. (See Tool 8-6 for a sample wallchart.)
  — a felt-tip marker for each team member.
* *For the instructor:*
  — an overhead transparency, PowerPoint slide, or flipchart page displaying the Players' Instructions.

Equipment:

* Overhead projector, or computer and projection/display monitor
* Flipchart with easel and felt-tipped markers to tally scores and post player comments and observations (optional).

Room Setup: Using easy-to-remove masking or painter's tape, hang up a wallchart for each team, leaving enough intervening wall space to avoid crowding. *Alternative:* Set up a flipchart on an easel for each team. Place one wallchart on each easel.

Tool 8-6: Sample Wallchart for Match Point

Theme Statement: "New Uses for Existing Products"

	C	S	W
_____ Cake mix			
_____ Liquid soap			
_____ Plastic bags			

Before Game Play:

1. Divide group into teams of three to seven players.
2. Have each team meet at one of the wallcharts.
3. Distribute a felt-tipped marker to each player.

How to Play the Game

1. Announce the theme. (For our example it's "New Uses for Existing Products.")
2. Announce the task: "Each team must brainstorm items suggested by a match of the letter and category. (In our example, an item for *cake mix* plus *C* might be *cookie mix;* an item for *plastic bags* plus *S* might be suit storage.)
3. Tell teams they have 10 minutes to brainstorm and list as many items as they can in each box as suggested by a match of letter and category. Start the clock.
4. Call time after 10 minutes.
5. Have each team select and then present to the whole class its three "most creative" entries.
6. Award two points for every item the individual teams have listed. Have teams tally and announce their point totals.
7. The team with the most points wins.

After Game Play—Debriefing:

Sample debriefing questions:

- How was it?
- What happened?
- What helped you brainstorm?
- What did you learn about yourself? About others?
- What helped you expand your ideas?
- How did your teammates help you?
- What did you learn about creativity?
- How will you apply these concepts back on the job?

Game Notes:

- Play in rounds. After the initial round of play, rotate teams to the next wallchart to see how many additional items they can create in five minutes. This reinforces the brainstorming concept of building on other's ideas.
- After the initial round of play, introduce wallcharts with new letters and categories. Usual results show an increase in items produced, a reflection on how practice increases brainstorming results.

PLAYERS' INSTRUCTIONS FOR
Match Point

1. Divide into teams of three or more players.

2. Each team receives a set of felt-tipped markers and meets at a wallchart.

3. Write in the spaces as many items as possible that are suggested by the categories and letters on the wallchart.

4. When time is called, tally the number of items written.

5. Receive two points for each item.

6. The team with the most points wins.

Title: Quiz Challenge

This is an all-purpose topic test-and-review game. Teams first estimate the number of questions they will answer correctly, and then respond to a set of questions. Interest peaks when the questions are reviewed by the instructor. The team that has the highest estimate of correct responses and meets or exceeds that estimate wins.

Format: Manual game

Overview:

Purpose: To reveal a learner's level of topic knowledge or understanding

Uses: Content application, interteam play, new content introduction, content review, vocabulary review, risk taking

Audience: Any level

Number of Players: 6 or more

Time Needed to Play Game: 20 to 40 minutes

Game Materials/Props:

- ◆ *For each team of two players:*
  - — 1 game sheet
    To make the game sheet: Prepare a set of 7 to 15 short-answer or multiple-choice questions on the topic (See Tool 8-7 for our example.)
  - — 1 pencil for each team member.
- ◆ *For the instructor:*
  - — a master sheet of your own notes and rationales, as well as the correct answers.

Equipment:

- ◆ Overhead projector, or computer and projection/display monitor
- ◆ Flipchart with easel and felt-tipped markers to tally scores and post player comments and observations (optional).

Room Setup: For best results, seat each team at its own table or gather teams in separate areas of the training room.

Before Game Play:

1. Divide the group into teams of two players.
2. Tell teams that they're going to take a short quiz and tell them how many questions there are in the quiz.
3. Ask each team to estimate how many correct responses it will make.
4. Post each team's estimate on the overhead transparency or flipchart.

Trainer's Tip:

It's easier to "batch" the estimates, such as: 6-7, 4-5, 0-3.

Tool 8-7: Sample Quiz Challenge Game Sheet

Estimated Correct Responses _____

Actual Correct Responses _____

1. According to time management expert Alan Lakein, what is the most common denominator among good time managers?

   a. They take advantage of waiting time.

   b. They have an established routine.

   c. They use a to-do list.

2. Experts report that it takes how many days of consistent behavior to establish a new routine?

   a. 14

   b. 21

   c. 35

3. "Batching," a time-saving technique, involves grouping similar tasks in the same time period. Give an example of batching tasks to save time:

   _____

4. When forced to interrupt a writing project, which of these techniques helps you get right back into the project flow when you return to it?

   a. writing in longhand

   b. stopping in the middle of a sentence

   c. noting "draft" on the top of the page

5. In ordinary circumstances, what is the maximum number of revisions you should make to the first draft of any document?

   a. 7

   b. 5

   c. 3

6. In business, how frequently is the average worker interrupted?

   a. every 6 to 9 minutes

   b. every 11 to 15 minutes

   c. every 17 to 21 minutes

7. In open offices or study areas, which kind of interruption is more disruptive?

   a. auditory

   b. visual

Answers:

1. c
2. b
3. batching return phone calls
4. b
5. c
6. a
7. b

Trainer's Tip:

Allow 60 to 90 seconds' response time for each question. Thus, for a seven-question quiz, the time allowed to take the quiz is 10 minutes

How to Play the Game:

1. Distribute one Quiz Challenge Sheet to each team.

2. Tell teams they have 10 minutes to finish the quiz. Start the clock.

3. Call time after 10 minutes, and go over the correct answers. Read aloud and, if possible, present each question on the overhead transparency or PowerPoint slide, and then present the correct answer. Give your rationale—the "why" this was the correct response—immediately. We have found that this is the time when players are very interested in the rationale behind the correct response.

4. Have each team announce its total number of correct answers.

5. The winning team is the one who had the highest estimate of correct answers *and* who met or exceeded that estimate.

After the Game—Debriefing:

Sample debriefing questions:

- How did it feel to make an estimate without knowing the nature of the questions?
- What helped you with your strategy?
- What did you experience?
- What did you observe?
- What helped you remember the content?
- Where did you see teamwork?
- How will you apply what you learned?

Game Notes:

- Allowing teams to self-score and tally their own correct responses can lead to post-game discussion on ethics, that is, "how far would you go to win?"

PLAYERS' INSTRUCTIONS FOR
Quiz Challenge

1. Divide into teams of two players.

2. Estimate the number of questions you will answer correctly.

3. Receive a copy of the quiz.

4. Answer as many questions as you can before time is called.

5. After the instructor reviews the quiz, tally the number of questions you answered correctly.

6. The team with the highest original estimate *and* whose score matches or exceeds its original estimate wins.

Game Plan: Working Checklist
Title:
Format:
Overview:
  Purpose:
  Use:
  Audience:
  Number of Players:
  Time Needed to Play Game:
Game Materials/Props:
Equipment:
Room Setup:
Before Game Play:

How to Play the Game:

After Game Play--Debriefing:

Title: Review Bingo

This is an excellent guide and review for home reading, handouts, and text material. Each team receives a bingo-style game sheet containing references to key items found in the text material. They scan their text or handouts to locate the required items. The team that covers the most game sheet spaces wins.

Format: Manual game

Overview:

Purpose: To review major learning points

Uses: New content introduction, content review, vocabulary review

Audience: Any level

Number of Players: 6 or more

Time Needed to Play Game: 20 to 30 minutes

Game Materials/Props:

- *For each team:*
  - 1 game sheet with 25 clues placed in a 5 x 5-space bingo-format layout (see Tool 8-8)
  - 1 pencil to mark the team's game sheet
  - 1 highlight marker to highlight text material (optional).

- *For the instructor:*
  - a master sheet of clues and the page number in the text or handout source containing the key information, and other notes as needed
  - a copy of the handout, text, or reading material associated with the game sheet
  - an overhead transparency, PowerPoint slide, or flipchart page displaying the Players' Instructions.

Trainer's Tip:

Game sheets comprising 25 clues placed on a 5 x 5-space layout can be prepared using the "Table" toolbar in Windows 2000 and up. Create a 5-row by 5-column table (auto-fit to window), and then fill in each space with your clues about key points found in the handout material or text.

Equipment:

- Overhead projector, or computer and projection/display monitor
- Flipchart with easel and felt-tipped markers to tally scores and post player comments and observations (optional).

Before Game Play:

1. Divide the group into teams of two or three players.
2. Distribute one game sheet, one copy of the text material, and one pencil to each team.

How to Play the Game:

1. Instruct teams that they have 15 minutes to locate items in the text material suggested by clues on the game sheet.

Tool 8-8: Review Bingo: Management Textbook Information Search

Gilbreth	McGregor	Synergy	Hawthorn Studies	Adams
Intrinsic	Weber	Maslow	Systems Theory	Feedback
Parker-Follett	Gantt	Closed System	Barnard	F.W. Taylor
Contingency	Theory Y	Extrinsic	Theory X	Open System
Fayol	Herzberg	Theory Z	McClelland	Blake and Mouton

Text material: *Management* by Richard L. Daft (Harcourt College Publishers, 2002)

2. When they find an item in the text material, they should mark an "X" through the space on the game sheet and write in that space the page number where the item was found.
3. Teams must locate as many items in the text material as they can.
4. Call time at 15 minutes.
5. The team with the most spaces covered wins.

After Game Play—Debriefing:

Sample debriefing questions:

- How was it?
- What did you enjoy the most?
- What did you learn about each other?
- What helped you work as a team?
- How will you apply what you have learned?
- What would you do differently next time?

PLAYERS' INSTRUCTIONS FOR
Review Bingo

1. Form teams of two or three players.

2. Each team receives a game sheet, text material, and a pencil.

3. When you find an item in the text that satisfies a specific clue on the game sheet:

   a. mark an "X" in the appropriate game sheet space

   b. write the text page where the item was found in that game sheet space.

4. Find as many text items as you can before time is called.

5. When time is called, the team with the most spaces covered wins.

Title: Sand Trap

This "floor game" is a terrific energizer— especially suited for use after a lunch break or to start off a day's training. Teams must solve a logic problem so that five team members may safely cross the floor grid (avoiding the "sand traps"). The game also features three levels of difficulty, and teams select their level of risk (and therefore the amount of gain they may realize). The team that scores the most points wins.

Format: Prop game

Overview:

Purposes: To create a team planning experience in conditions of risk; to demonstrate the relationship between proper planning and payoff

Uses: Icebreaker, interteam play, problem solving, risk taking, team learning

Audience: Any level, but especially suited to new or existing work teams

Number of Players: 5 or more

Time Needed to Play Game: 25 to 50 minutes

Game Materials/Props:

❖ *For each team:*

— 1 pad of sticky-notes

— 1 broad highlighter to mark the planning grid

— 1 clue-and-planning sheet for one of three levels (low, moderate, and high), which gives a set of general instructions; a planning grid that provides a "practice field" where teams may plot out a crossing, noting which spaces are safe and which spaces contain sand traps; and the clues for identifying the sand trap locations:

  • risk level 1 (low) provides all necessary clues, but awards the fewest points for safe passage (7)

  • risk level 2 (moderate) provides most of the clues and awards 15 points for safe passage

  • risk level 3 (high) provides some of the clues, but awards a whopping 25 points for safe passage.

See Tools 8-9, 8-10, and 8-11, on pages 105, 106, and 107.

  ◆ *For the instructor:*

  — 1 roll of masking or painter's tape (preferably colored or patterned tape, and one that's low-tack so no floors are damaged) or large chalk sticks to create a floor grid

  — 2 sheets of colored paper, preferably yellow or orange

  — a 30-second timer (audible, if possible)

  — a master sheet (see Tool 8-12 as an example)

  — an overhead transparency, PowerPoint slide, or flipchart page displaying the Players' Instructions; the same materials may be used to display the clear path when all teams have had their turns.

Equipment:

  ◆ Overhead projector, or computer and projection/display monitor

  ◆ Flipchart with easel and felt-tipped markers to tally scores, or post player comments and observations (optional).

Room Setup:

  ◆ Prepare your floor grid (this usually takes 15-20 minutes). First, clear an area of floor space that is 10 feet square. Using masking or painter's tape (or chalk), follow these steps to lay out a 5 x 5-space floor grid:

  1. Outline a 10-foot square on the floor.

  2. Place four 10-foot strips of tape (or draw chalk lines) horizontally at 2-foot intervals.

3. Place four 10-foot pieces of tape (or chalk lines) vertically at 2-foot intervals.

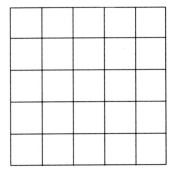

4. Label one yellow or orange sheet "Start" and label the other sheet "Finish."
5. Tape the two sheets at the appropriate places on the floor grid.
6. For best results, provide a table and chairs for each team.

Before Game Play:

1. Divide the group into teams of five or six players each.
2. Tell teams they must use the logic-problem clues provided on their clue-and-planning sheets to identify the locations of sand traps on the floor grid, and then send five players safely across the grid without stepping into any of those sand traps.
3. The clues are batched at three risk levels and each team will select its own risk level—
   a. low risk level (1), which provides *all* the clues they need for a safe crossing, but with the fewest scoring points (7)
   b. moderate risk level (2), which provides *most* of the clues they need for crossing, with 15 points for completing the crossing safely
   c. high risk level (3), which provides *some* of the clues they need for crossing, and with the most points for success (25).
4. Explain that the first player to cross will place a sticky-note in each safe square of the floor grid to define the path for the other four team members who will cross. Those four players then must cross the grid following that path.
5. Also tell players that each team will receive one crossing point for every second less than 30 it takes to mark the safe path and send its players across without stepping in a sand trap.

How to Play the Game

1. Each team meets to choose the risk level of its clue-and-planning sheet.
2. After receiving the clue-and-planning sheet, each team has 10 minutes to plan its crossing. During this time, each team must
   a. plot a safe crossing of the floor grid
   b. select its first player and four crossing team members.

3. After 10 minutes, the trainer selects the first crossing team. (Choose the team with the lowest risk as the first crossing team and then work up to the team with the highest risk level. We suggest doing it in this order because if the team with the highest risk level team is the first to safely cross the grid, the number of points they gain at that level [25] removes all suspense of who will win.)

4. Ask the nonplaying teams to leave the room.

5. Have the first player and the rest of the crossing team line up single-file at the starting line.

6. Start the 30-second clock. The first member crosses the grid, placing sticky-notes to identify a safe crossing path. Then, one by one, the next four team members cross the floor grid.

7. If any player steps on a sand trap, the team is immediately disqualified.

8. If all five team members safely cross the floor grid, the team receives the number of points available for the level of risk it assumed (low = 7, moderate = 15, high = 25), and 1 crossing point for each second less than 30 it took the five members to cross the grid.

9. The first team takes its seats. The next team is invited into the room and takes its turn crossing the grid.

10. Play continues until all teams have crossed the grid.

11. The team with the most points wins.

After Game Play—Debriefing:

Sample debriefing questions:

- How did it go?
- What was your biggest "aha!"?
- What helped your team?
- What hindered your team?
- How willing was your team to take a risk?
- What did your learn about planning?
- What would you do differently?
- How will you apply some of these concepts back at work?

Game Notes:

- Print the clue-and-planning sheets in three different colors, according to risk level, for easy identification during distribution and game play.
- Appoint one or two assistants to help you
  — monitor the grid crossing
  — measure the time each team takes to cross the grid.
- Use a noisemaker (hand bell, whistle) to signal the start and finish of each crossing.

Tool 8-9: Sand Trap Clue-and-Planning Sheet, Level I

General Information

* The floor grid contains 25 spaces; **9** spaces are sand traps.
* **Clues** are in three formats:
  — by **space number,** as labeled in your grid illustration below
  — by **columns** (a vertical line of spaces, such as 1, 6, 11, 16, 21); columns are numbered left to right (first column = 1–21, second column = 2–22, and so forth)
  — by **rows** (a horizontal line of spaces, such as 1, 2, 3, 4, 5); rows are numbered bottom to top (first row = 1-5, second row = 6-10, and so forth).
* You must **enter the floor grid** through a first-row space—1, 2, 3, 4, or 5.
* **Entering any sand trap space** immediately disqualifies your team.
* **No diagonal moves are allowed**—you must cross the grid one **horizontal or vertical** space at a time. For example, to move from space 1 to space 7, you could move horizontally from space 1 to space 2 and then vertically from space 2 to space 7.
* You must **exit the grid** from a fifth-row space—21, 22, 23, 24, or 25.

FINISH LINE

21	22	23	24	25
16	17	18	19	20
11	12	13	14	15
6	7	8	9	10
1	2	3	4	5

STARTING LINE

Clue List: Low Risk Level

* There are 2 sand traps in the first row.
* There is 1 sand trap in the fifth column.
* The four corner spaces are clear.
* There are 3 sand traps in the third column.
* There is 1 sand trap in the second row.
* Space #2 is clear.
* There are 2 sand traps in the fourth column.
* There are 3 sand traps in the fifth row.
* Space #12 is clear.
* There are 3 sand traps in the third row.
* There is 1 sand trap in the first column.
* Space #14 is clear.
* There are 2 sand traps in the second column.
* There are no sand traps in the fourth row.
* Space #7 is a sand trap.

Tool 8-10: Sand Trap Clue-and-Planning Sheet, Level 2

General Information

◆ The floor grid contains 25 spaces; **9** spaces are sand traps.

◆ **Clues** are in three formats:

— by **space number,** as labeled in your grid illustration below

— by **columns** (a vertical line of spaces, such as 1, 6, 11, 16, 21); columns are numbered left to right (first column = 1-21, second column = 2-22, and so forth)

— by **rows** (a horizontal line of spaces, such as 1, 2, 3, 4, 5); rows are numbered bottom to top (first row = 1-5, second row = 6-10, and so forth).

◆ You must **enter the floor grid** through a first-row space—1, 2, 3, 4, or 5.

◆ **Entering any sand trap space** immediately disqualifies your team.

◆ **No diagonal moves are allowed**—you must cross the grid one **horizontal or vertical** space at a time. For example, to move from space 1 to space 7, you could move horizontally from space 1 to space 2 and then vertically from space 2 to space 7.

◆ You must **exit the grid** from a fifth-row space—21, 22, 23, 24, or 25.

FINISH LINE ⟵ ⟶

21	22	23	24	25
16	17	18	19	20
11	12	13	14	15
6	7	8	9	10
1	2	3	4	5

⟵ STARTING LINE ⟶

Clue List: Moderate Risk Level

◆ There are 2 sand traps in the first row.

◆ There is 1 sand trap in the fifth column.

◆ There are 3 sand traps in the third column.

◆ There is 1 sand trap in the second row.

◆ Space #14 is clear.

◆ There are 2 sand traps in the fourth column.

◆ There are 3 sand traps in the fifth row.

◆ Space #7 is a sand trap.

◆ There are 3 sand traps in the third row.

◆ The four corner spaces are clear.

Tool 8-11: Sand Trap Clue-and-Planning Sheet, Level 3

General Information

- The floor grid contains 25 spaces; **9** spaces are sand traps.
- **Clues** are in three formats:
  - by **space number,** as labeled in your grid illustration below
  - by **columns** (a vertical line of spaces, such as 1, 6, 11, 16, 21); columns are numbered left to right (first column = 1-21, second column = 2-22, and so forth)
  - by **rows** (a horizontal line of spaces, such as 1, 2, 3, 4, 5); rows are numbered bottom to top (first row = 1-5, second row = 6-10, and so forth).
- You must **enter the floor grid** through a first-row space—1, 2, 3, 4, or 5.
- **Entering any sand trap space** immediately disqualifies your team.
- **No diagonal moves are allowed**—you must cross the grid one **horizontal or vertical** space at a time. For example, to move from space 1 to space 7, you could move horizontally from space 1 to space 2 and then vertically from space 2 to space 7.
- You must **exit the grid** from a fifth-row space—21, 22, 23, 24, or 25.

← FINISH LINE →

21	22	23	24	25
16	17	18	19	20
11	12	13	14	15
6	7	8	9	10
1	2	3	4	5

← STARTING LINE →

Clue List: High Risk Level

- There is 1 sand trap in the fifth column.
- The four corner spaces are clear.
- There are 3 sand traps in the third row.
- There are 2 sand traps in the fourth column.
- There are 3 sand traps in the fifth row.
- Spaces #4 and #7 are sand traps.

Tool 8-12: Facilitator's Sample Sand Trap Solution Sheet

FINISH LINE

21	22 ST	23 ST	24 ST	25
16	17	18	19	20
11 ST	12	13 ST	14	15 ST
6	7 ST	8	9	10
1	2	3 ST	4 ST	5

STARTING LINE

ST = Sand trap

= Suggested path

PLAYERS' INSTRUCTIONS FOR
Sand Trap

1. Divide into teams of five or six players.

2. Select a clue-and-planning sheet based on risk level:

   a. low risk (provides all clues needed), earns 7 points

   b. moderate risk (provides most clues needed), earns 15 points

   c. high risk (provides some clues), earns 25 points.

3. You have 10 minutes to plan for five players to safely cross the grid.

4. The first player lays out a safe path with sticky notes; other four players follow that path to cross safely. Stepping on a sand trap disqualifies the team.

5. Scoring: If all team members safely cross the grid they receive the points offered by the risk level they chose *plus* one crossing point for each second less than 30 it took the five team members to cross safely.

6. The team with the most points wins.

Title: Signature Hunt

This icebreaker requires players to get signatures from other players to match the descriptions on their game sheets. The descriptive terms usually reflect the characteristics or backgrounds of members of the class. The player who covers the most game sheet spaces wins. (You may also adapt this game to reflect the topic, as demonstrated in Tool 8-13.)

Format: Manual game

Overview:

Purpose: To introduce the class members to one another and to the trainer

Uses: Icebreaker

Audience: Any level

Number of Players: 6 or more

Time Needed to Play Game: 15 to 30 minutes

Game Materials/Props:

- *For each player:*
  - 1 game sheet with 25 clues placed in a 5 x 5-space bingo-format layout (Keep the clue descriptions as short as possible to encourage brief fact-finding dialogues between participants.)
  - 1 pencil or marker for each player.
- *For the instructor:*
  - a master sheet of clues and other notes as needed
  - an overhead transparency, PowerPoint slide, or flipchart page displaying the Players' Instructions.

Equipment:

- Overhead projector, or computer and projection/display monitor
- Flipchart with easel and felt-tipped markers to tally scores and record player comments and observations (optional).

Room Setup: No special setup is required, but it is helpful if players have enough space to meet and talk with other players.

Before Game Play:

- Distribute a game sheet and pencil to each player.

Trainer's Tip:

Game sheets of 25 clues placed on a 5 x 5-space layout can be prepared using the "Table" toolbar in Windows 2000 and up. Create a five-row by five-column table (auto-fit to window), and fill in each space with your clue about a personal trait or characteristic of the class or a clue about the topic.

Tool 8-13: Sample Signature Hunt Game Sheet—Find Someone Who . . .

Has read a book or article on meeting management	Has a sweet-tooth	Jogs or exercises on a regular basis	Usually eats lunch at her or his desk	Is mechanically inclined
Works in human resources	Has taken a workshop in stress management	Has read a book or article on time management	Is artistic	Is a gardener
Has two or more pets	Has a cluttered desk	Goes to school at night or on weekends	Knits, quilts, or weaves	Plays a musical instrument
Is good at multitasking	Has a Website	Was born west of the Mississippi River	Currently uses a to do list	Likes to ski or snowboard
Regularly backs up his or her computer files	Likes to do crossword puzzles	Does financial analysis or budget work	Has run for political office	Regularly takes work home

How to Play the Game

1. Announce the task: "Each player must get the signatures of other players who meet the requirements described in the spaces on the game sheet."

2. Players mingle as a group, seeking people who match the descriptions. When a match is found, that person signs the seeker's appropriate space.

3. Depending on time and/or group members, choose among these possible winning patterns:
   — covering five-in-a-row (vertically, horizontally, or corner-to-corner)
   — covering all exterior spaces (sometimes called the picture frame)
   — covering all nine interior spaces (sometimes called a nine-pack)
   — covering all game sheet spaces (a "black out" or "full house").

After Game Play—Debriefing:

Sample debriefing questions:

- What did you learn about others in the room?
- What did you experience?
- What happened?
- What did you learn?
- How will you apply this?

Game Note:

- With larger groups, allow players to obtain only one signature from any other player. This will encourage mingling.

PLAYERS' INSTRUCTIONS FOR
Signature Hunt

1. Each player receives a game sheet.

2. Players must find other players who meet the descriptions on the game sheet.

3. When you find a player who qualifies, get him or her to sign the appropriate clue on the game sheet.

4. When time is called, the player with the most signed spaces wins.

Title: Tic-Tac-Topic

Because of its universal recognition and play, this game can be introduced wherever and whenever you need to review content. Simply pair up your students and start your game: A player selects a game sheet space and then must answer a topic question to earn that space. Play alternates back and forth until one of the players wins by covering three spaces in a row.

Format: Manual game

Overview:

Purpose: To reveal a learner's level of topic knowledge or understanding

Uses: Content application, new content introduction, content review, vocabulary review

Audience: Any level

Number of Players: 6 or more

Time Needed to Play Game: 10 to 20 minutes

Game Materials/Props:

♦ *For each team:*

— 1 game sheet (Game sheets contain the standard 3 x 3-space tic-tac-toe grid and players can draw it quickly on blank paper if you don't wish to prepare the grids in advance.)

— 1 token (coin, button, wrapped candy, golf tee) per game sheet

— 1 pencil or marker.

♦ *For the instructor:*

— a list of 10 to 15 short-answer questions to be presented orally (As an alternative you may present the questions on an overhead transparency, a PowerPoint slide, or on flipchart pages.)

— a master sheet of answers and other notes as needed

— an overhead transparency, PowerPoint slide, or flipchart page displaying the Players' Instructions.

Equipment:

♦ Overhead projector, or computer and projection/display monitor

♦ Flipchart with easel and felt-tipped markers to tally scores and post player comments and observations (optional).

Room Setup: For best results, provide a table and chairs for each team of two players.

Before Game Play:

1. Divide the group into pairs of players.
2. Ask players to decide who will be player "X" and who will be player "O."
3. Distribute sheets of paper and pencils, and instruct each pair to draw a 3 x 3-space tic-tac-toe grid on the paper:

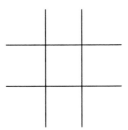

4. Give one token to each set of players.

How to Play the Game:

1. Have player X select a space on the grid by placing a token on that space.
2. Trainer asks or presents the first question.
3. Player X has 15 seconds to give his or her response to player O.
4. If the answer is correct, player X removes the token and marks "X" in the space. If the answer is incorrect, the token is removed and player X's turn is over.
5. Player O selects a space, places the token in that space, and answers the next question.
6. Play continues in this fashion—Player X marking earned spaces with an "X," Player "O" marking earned spaces with an "O"—until one player covers three spaces in a row, horizontally, vertically, or diagonally.
7. If no player covers three in a row, then the player with the most spaces covered when time elapses is declared the winner.

After Game Play—Debriefing:

Sample debriefing questions:

- How was it?
- What happened?
- What did you experience?
- What did you observe that helped you answer the questions?
- What strategies were helpful to you?
- What questions are you still thinking about?
- How will you apply what you learned?

Game Notes:

- As an alternative, conduct a "time-driven" game—when time is called, the player with the most covered spaces wins.
- As an alternative, allow a player to cover the center space *only* if she or he correctly answers two questions.
- As an alternative, divide class into two sections—left side of the room and right side, or men and women—and have the sections compete against one another.

PLAYERS' INSTRUCTIONS FOR
Tic-Tac-Topic

1. Divide into sets of two players—one player is "X," the other player is "O."

2. Player X chooses a space and places the token there.

3. Player X responds to the first question.

4. If the response is correct, player X removes the token and places an "X" in the space.

5. If the response is incorrect, player X removes the token.

6. Player O chooses a space, places the token, and responds to a question.

7. Play continues until one player covers three spaces in a row, horizontally, vertically, or diagonally.

Title: Toss Up

This is an exciting qualify-and-score game in which teams answer topic questions to earn target throws (for points). The team with the most points wins.

Format: Prop game

Overview:

Purpose: To review major learning points

Uses: Content application, interteam play, content review, vocabulary review, risk taking, team learning

Audience: Any level

Number of Players: 8 or more

Time Needed to Play Game: 25 to 70 minutes

Game Materials/Props:

- *For each team:*
    - 1 pencil
    - 1 game sheet of five questions for each round (see Tool 8-14 for our example—including the answers FYI)
    To create the game sheet: Create questions similar to your normal exam questions—short answer, multiple choice, or true-false. Print one quiz per sheet of paper. If possible, print each round's quiz on different-colored paper so it's easier to track and manage game play.

- *For the instructor:*
    - 1 soup bowl target (4-5" wide, 2-3" deep)
    - double-sided tape, to attach soup bowl to target table
    - 5 Koosh balls, beanbags, or other soft throwing objects
    - masking or painter's tape, preferably brightly colored or patterned, to create a throw line 4 feet from the target table
    - stopwatch or timer (optional)
    - noisemaker or chimes to signal that time is up (optional).

Equipment:

- 1 conference table to hold the target bowl
- Overhead projector, or computer and projection/display monitor
- Flipchart with easel and felt-tipped markers to tally scores, and post player comments and observations (optional).

Tool 8-14: Sample Toss Up Game Sheet

Team _____ Round No. _____

Topic: Stress Management

1. What is the daily amount of water your body needs to function well—four, six, or eight glasses?
2. What is the top source of fat in women's diets—margarine, salad dressing, or cheese?
3. What is the most frequently consumed source of caffeine in the American diet? _____
4. What is the only way to use the stress hormones once they are released into your body—meditation, deep breathing, or exercise?
5. Rest is the only thing that restores the wear and tear on your body— true or false?

Answers:

1. Eight glasses. About two quarts is OK for the average person; more if you are over-weight.
2. Salad dressing, according to the U.S. Department of Agriculture. Try no-oil or yogurt dressings as an alternative.
3. Coffee. Americans over the age of 14 consume an average of three cups per day.
4. Exercise. The stress hormones put your body in an alert state of readiness. After exercising you will soon be able to relax.
5. True. Whereas a proper diet fuels your body's machine by giving you needed energy, adequate rest rejuvenates you and helps you deal with your day.

Room Setup:

- For best results, provide a table and chairs for each team.
- Place the target 12 inches from the throwing edge of the conference table.
- Create a throw line on the floor next to the conference table by placing a 3-foot strip of masking or painter's tape four feet from the edge of the table that holds the target bowl.

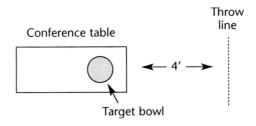

Before Game Play:

- Divide the group into two to four teams of four to seven players.

How to Play the Game:

1. Give a five-question game sheet to each team. Tell players they have three minutes to answer the questions.
2. Call time after three minutes, collect game sheets, and go over the correct answers.
3. Award one target throw for each correct response.
4. Each team meets and selects a thrower. Teams may ask for a volunteer or select a player, usually an "athletic" type who may appear to have the best chance of making the target throw.
5. The designated thrower takes the number of target throws earned by the team in answering questions.
6. Each toss into the bowl earns 3 points; tosses that land anywhere else earn no points.
7. Play subsequent rounds in the same way, using the other game sheets with different question sets on them. The team with the most points at the end of all rounds wins.

After Game Play—Debriefing:

Sample debriefing questions:

- What happened?
- What did you experience?
- What did you observe during game play?
- How will you apply what you have learned?

Game Note:

- *Alternate question format:* Distribute blank quiz game sheets and display the questions for each round on overhead transparencies or on PowerPoint slides.

PLAYERS' INSTRUCTIONS FOR
Toss Up

1. Divide into two or more teams.

2. The game is played in rounds. In every round, each team has three minutes to answer the five questions on that round's game sheet.

3. Each team receives one target throw for each correct response.

4. One player on each team makes the team's earned tosses at the target.

5. Each team receives three points for every toss that lands in the target. No points are earned if the toss lands elsewhere.

6. Play continues until all rounds are completed, and the team with the most points at the end of the final round wins.

Using the Compact Disc

The compact disc that accompanies this book on training games contains files that can be used on a variety of computer platforms. The files are Adobe .pdf documents.

To read or print the .pdf files on the CD, you must have Adobe Acrobat Reader software installed on your system. The program can be downloaded free of cost from the Adobe Website, www.adobe.com.

To print the training materials using Adobe Acrobat Reader, simply open a .pdf file and print as many copies as you need. You can print them on paper to use as handouts, or on transparencies to use on your overhead projector.

The following .pdf documents can be directly printed from the CD:

* Chart 1-1: The Costs and Benefits of Games in Your Training
* Checklist 1-1: Ten Questions to Ask and Answer Before Using a Training Game
* Figure 6-1: The Four Stages of Kolb's Experiential Learning Cycle
* Figure 6-2: Learning Styles within the Context of Kolb's Experiential Learning Cycle
* Players' Instructions—Bingo Hunt
* Players' Instructions—Board Bingo
* Players' Instructions—Card Sort
* Players' Instructions—Get-Set
* Players' Instructions—Match Point
* Players' Instructions—Quiz Challenge
* Players' Instructions—Review Bingo
* Players' Instructions—Sand Trap
* Players' Instructions—Signature Hunt

- Players' Instructions—Tic-Tac-Topic
- Players' Instructions—Toss Up
- Tool 2-1: Group Size Adaptation Chart
- Tool 3-1: Game Plan: Working Checklist
- Tool 6-1: Facilitator Responsibilities Chart
- Tool 6-2: Applying the Experiential Learning Cycle to Games
- Tool 6-3: Typical Behaviors Associated with Learning Styles
- Tool 7-1: Sample Debriefing Questions for Each Stage of the Experiential Learning Cycle
- Tool 7-2: Managing Group Dynamics
- Tool 8-1: Game Use Matrix
- Tool 8-2: Sample Bingo Hunt Game Sheet
- Tool 8-3: Board Bingo Game Board
- Tool 8-3A: Four-Color Board Bingo Game Board
- Tool 8-4: Sample Card Sort Chart and Item Cards
- Tool 8-5: Sample Get-Set Game Sheet
- Tool 8-6: Sample Wallchart for Match Point
- Tool 8-7: Sample Quiz Challenge Game Sheet
- Tool 8-8: Sample Review Bingo Game Sheet: Management Textbook Information Search
- Tool 8-9: Sand Trap Clue-and-Planning Sheet, Level 1
- Tool 8-10: Sand Trap Clue-and-Planning Sheet, Level 2
- Tool 8-11: Sand Trap Clue-and-Planning Sheet, Level 3
- Tool 8-12: Facilitator's Sample Sand Trap Solution Sheet
- Tool 8-13: Sample Signature Hunt Game Sheet—Find Someone Who . . .
- Tool 8-14: Sample Toss Up Game Sheet

Resources

Books

Beich, Elaine. 2005. *Training for Dummies*. Hoboken, NJ: Wiley.

Clark, Ruth Colvin. 1989. *Developing Technical Training*. Phoenix, AZ: Buzzards Bay Press

Kolb, David A. 1984. *Experiential Learning: Experience as the Source of Learning and Development*. Englewood Cliffs, NJ: Prentice Hall

Koppett, Kat. 2001. *Training to Imagine*. Sterling, VA: Stylus Press.

Lawson, Karen. 1998. *The Trainer's Handbook* San Francisco: Jossey-Bass/Pfeiffer.

Newstrom, John W., and Edward E. Scannel. 1980. *Games Trainers Play* New York: McGraw-Hill.

———. 1998. *The Big Book of Team Building Games: Trust-Building Activities, Team Spirit Exercises, and Other Fun Things to Do*. New York: McGraw-Hill.

Preziosi, Robert C. 1999. *Icebreakers*. Alexandria, VA: ASTD Press, Infoline.

Russell, Lou. 1999. *The Accelerated Learning Fieldbook*. San Francisco: Jossey-Bass/Pfeiffer.

Silberman, Mel. 1990. *Active Training*. New York: Lexington Books.

Smith, Donna M., and David A. Kolb. 1986. *The User's Guide for the Learning-Style Inventory*. Boston: McBer & Company.

Sugar, Steve. 1998. *Games That Teach*. San Francisco: Jossey-Bass/Pfeiffer.

———. 2000. *More Great Games*. Alexandria, VA: ASTD Press, Infoline.

Sugar, Steve, and George Takacs. 2000. *Games That Teach Teams*. San Francisco: Jossey-Bass/Pfeiffer.

Sugar, Steve, and Carol Willett. 2004. *Games That Boost Performance*. San Francisco: Jossey-Bass/Pfeiffer.

Thiagarajan, Sivasailam. 2003. *Design Your Own Games and Activities*. San Francisco: Jossey-Bass/Pfeiffer.

Ukens, Lorraine. 2001. *What Smart Trainers Know*. San Francisco: Jossey-Bass/Pfeiffer.

West, Edie. 1996. *201 Icebreakers*. New York: McGraw-Hill.

———. 1999. *Big Book of Icebreakers*. New York: McGraw-Hill.

Articles

Baker, Ann C., Patricia J. Jensen, and David A. Kolb. 1997. "In Conversation: Transforming Experience into Learning." *Simulation and Gaming* 28(1): 6-11.

Kolb, David A., Richard E. Boystris, and Charalampos Mainemelis. 1999. "Experiential Learning Theory—Previous Research and New Directions." Department of Organizational Behavior, Weatherhead School of Management, Case Western Reserve University, Cleveland, OH.

Leek, James E., and Bill Watson. 1996. "What Is the Experiential Learning Cycle?" Program in Intercultural Management, School for International Training, Brattleboro, VT.

Peters, Vincent A. M., and Geert A. N. Vissers. 2004. "A Simple Classification Model for Debriefing Simulation Games." Simulation and Gaming 35(1): 70-84.

Sugar, Steve. 2000. "Using Games to Energize Dry Material." In George M. Piskurich, Peter Beckschi, and Brandon Hall, eds., *The ASTD Handbook of Training Design and Delivery.* New York: McGraw-Hill.

Sugar, Steve, and C. Willett. 1994. "The Game of Academic Ethics: The Partnering of a Board Game." *To Improve the Academy,* volume 13. Ft. Collins, CO: Professional & Organizational Development Network in Higher Education.

Thiagarajan, Sivasailam. 2001. "Training Games and Activities." In Lorraine, Ukens, ed., *What Smart Trainers Know.* San Francisco: Jossey-Bass/Pfeiffer.

Ulrich, Markus. 1997. "Links Between Experiential Learning and Simulation and Gaming." In Jac Guerts, Sisca Joldersma, and Ellie Roelofs, eds., Gaming/Simulation for Policy Development and Organizational Change. Proceedings of the 28th Annual International Conference of the International Simulation and Gaming Association, Tilburg, The Netherlands, July 1997.

Training Websites

www.astd.org—Publications concerning and services useful for training

www.bobpikegroup.com—Publications and presentation products

www.hrdq.com—Products and activities

www.nasaga.org—Publications and resources focusing on training games

www.performanceexpress.org—Articles about and services for training

www.thegamegroup.com—Game products and publications

www.thiagi.com—Publications, newsletter, game products, and services

www.trainerswarehouse.com—Books, training games, and accessories

www.trainingmag.com—Training publications and services

About the Authors

Steve Sugar writes "fun with a purpose" activities that, every year, help thousands of learners experience classroom topics in a more meaningful way. He is the author or co-author of these four Jossey-Bass books: *Games That Teach Teams, Games That Boost Performance, Primary Games,* and *Games That Teach.* He has also written *More Great Games* for the ASTD Infoline. Sugar has developed three game systems featured by Langevin Learning Services: the *Learn It* board game, the *QUIZO* bingo game, and the *X-O Cise* dice game.

Sugar is on the business management faculty at the University of Maryland, Baltimore County, and has made numerous presentations at international conferences hosted by ASTD, the Association for Supervision and Curriculum Development, the International Society for Performance Improvement, the North American Simulation and Gaming Association, and *Training* magazine.

His games and design techniques are featured in a variety of books and journals, including *The Consultant's Big Book of Organization Development Tools: 50 Reproducible Intervention Tools to Help Solve Your Clients' Problems* (McGraw-Hill, 2003), *The 2001 Annual* (Jossey-Bass/Pfeiffer), *The ASTD Handbook of Training Design and Delivery* (McGraw-Hill, 2000), *The ASTD Handbook of Instructional Technology* (McGraw-Hill, 1993), *The Team and Organization Development Sourcebook* (McGraw-Hill, 1999, 2003), *Creative New Employee Orientation Programs* (McGraw-Hill, 2002), *The Training and Performance Sourcebook* (McGraw-Hill, 2000, 2004), *The Consultant's Big Book of Organization Development Tools* (McGraw-Hill, 2003), and *To Improve the Academy: Resources for Faculty, Instructional, & Organizational Development* (New Forums Press, 1994).

Sugar earned his undergraduate degree at Bucknell University (Pennsylvania) and his master's in business administration at George Washington University (Washington, D.C.). He served as a Coast Guard officer in Vietnam. Today he can be reached by email at info@thegamegroup.com. His Website is www.thegamegroup.com.

Jennifer Whitcomb, principal of the Trillium Group, is an experienced training and organization development practitioner with private sector and public sector clients in Asia, Canada, Europe, Latin America, and the United States.

She has helped more than 3,500 new and practiced trainers enhance their instructional design and facilitation skills by implementing performance-based, learner-centered techniques that create engagement, interest, and retention. She also has performed activities to improve team effectiveness, coached leaders to reach their goals, and facilitated outcome-oriented meetings and retreats.

Whitcomb is a previous director of Georgetown University's Organization Development Certificate Program. She helped new consultants apply and leverage tools and techniques to enhance organization effectiveness.

She has made presentations on effective training and consulting techniques at numerous international conferences, including those sponsored by ASTD and the Organizational Development Network.

Whitcomb earned her master of arts degree and an Advanced Instructional Design Certificate from Marymount University (Virginia). She holds a bachelor of arts degree in psychology from York University (Toronto, Ontario). She also holds the Professional Certified Coach designation through the International Coach Federation.

Whitcomb can be reached by email at jcwhitcomb@thetrilliumgroup.com, and her Website is www.thetrilliumgroup.com.